OUR MIGHTY
FORTRESS

OUR MIGHTY FORTRESS

FINDING REFUGE IN GOD

JOAN ESHERICK

Scripture taken from the *Holy Bible, New International Version*® NIV®. Copyright © 1973, 1978, 1984 by International Bible Society. Used by permission of Zondervan Publishing House. All rights reserved.

Scripture quotations marked NASB are taken from the *New American Standard Bible,*® © Copyright The Lockman Foundation 1960, 1962, 1963, 1968, 1971, 1972, 1973, 1975, 1977, 1995. Used by permission.

ISBN: 0-8024-1149-5

1 3 5 7 9 10 8 6 4 2

Printed in the United States of America

To my husband, Don.

My best friend and lover,

my spiritual head and counselor,

my beloved companion for the journey.

And to my children, Dan, Sarah, and Jon.

God's gracious gifts all,

without whom I would never have known

the joy of refuge in God.

CONTENTS

ACKNOWLEDGMENTS

I am greatly indebted to the following family, friends, colleagues, and ministry partners for their help, support, and encouragement:

Vicki Fitzgerald, who proofread my drafts. Her faithful prayer and attention to detail helped produce a stronger manuscript. Thanks, V!

Jeff Supp, pastor of adult ministries at Calvary Church in Souderton, Pennsylvania, who read my drafts for theological accuracy. Thank you, Jeff, for keeping me focused.

My twin sister, Jean Ford, whose memory is far better than mine. Thanks, Jeanie, for verifying my recollections, and, as always, for being there.

Elsa Mazon, acquisitions manager at Moody Press. I'm delighted to find not only a colleague in you, Elsa, but a kindred spirit and friend. Your passion for God, heart for women's ministry, and desire to communicate truth in a warm, inviting way have encouraged and inspired me. It's been a joy to work together.

Jim Vincent, general editor at Moody Press. Thank you, Jim, for your grace, patience, insight, and skill. Your careful editing has produced a polished, more readable work, and I'm grateful. It's been a privilege to learn from and work with you.

The rest of the Moody Press team. Thank you, all, for your support and investment in this project. I am especially indebted to Joe Ragont for bringing this book's castle imagery to life. Your work has enabled us to visualize the Mighty Fortress of God.

And of course, thanks to my dear husband, Don, and our kids, Dan, Sarah, and Jon, whose love, support, patience, sacrifice, and willingness to pitch in around the house made it possible for me to write. I could never have done this without you. Thanks, guys! I love you.

I am also deeply grateful to the God of this Fortress—for His grace in Jesus Christ and for His presence and provision throughout the writing of this book. He has been my refuge through it all.

INTRODUCTION:
Finding the Refuge

As I write these words, I'm coming off of months of nonstop demands on my time and energy: the holidays (those are demanding enough!), birthdays, anniversaries, two deaths in the family, a heavy teaching schedule, writing deadlines, speaking engagements, and major snowstorms. Couple these with parenting three teenagers, struggling with seasonal depression, dealing with SATs and college visitations, having a husband who travels on business, laundry that won't wash itself, and a house that just can't manage to keep itself clean, and, you guessed it: I'm worn out.

Emotionally, physically, mentally, spiritually—you name it, I'm spent. I need refuge.

Needing refuge isn't new to me. It's something I've experienced through years of struggling with the pressures and heartaches of everyday life. God is merciful, however, and has enabled me to find satisfying refuge for my soul. This "finding" has been a journey for me: a journey through my longing into the waiting arms of God. The journey has, at times, been long and arduous, fraught with wrong turns and side trips (my prayer is that it need not be so for you), but it has ultimately been a grace-filled journey framed by God's loving sovereignty.

My journey began in January 1984. Happily married, supporting my husband in seminary, and pregnant with my first child—life was all I hoped it would be. God was good, and we felt His blessing. Then, thirty-seven weeks into my pregnancy, I went into labor. Meconium in my water and a dropping fetal heart rate meant that something was wrong: My unborn baby was in distress.

As I anxiously delivered Daniel and listened for his first, plaintive cries I was confused by the unexpected quiet of the delivery room. The doctors and nurses exchanged concerned, silent glances while I strained to deliver the placenta. *It's not supposed to be this hard,* I remember thinking. *Delivering the placenta is supposed to be easy.* My husband's near fainting confirmed my escalating fear. He saw what I suspected: I had delivered a second son, Daniel's twin brother, and that son was stillborn.

In the midst of my confusion and heartbreak, I heard Daniel's first cries. I wanted desperately to hold my living child, but my longing went unfulfilled as nurses whisked Daniel from my waiting arms to the neonatal intensive care unit. Not only had I lost a son, but my surviving son had had a stroke, and was left with cerebral palsy.

Aching with concern and fearing the future, I longed for a sense that all would be well. I desperately needed a place of security and peace. Where would I flee? I ran to the Land of Silver Linings. Convinced that God would use Daniel's mind to compensate for his physical challenges, I sought refuge there.

Year after year, my hope increased as I saw Daniel's growing intelligence blossom. Astutely observant, quick-witted, and having a delightful sense of humor, he progressed wonderfully—until he started school. We soon discovered that our inquisitive son had multiple learning disabilities, and my hope for his academic success vanished.

OK, I thought. *His body may not be normal, and learning will be hard, but he's such a social guy. God will certainly use his social ability to see him through.* Heartbroken and weary, I inwardly fled to another silver lining: God's ability to use Daniel's character and personality. Again, I was disappointed. My well-liked son began having seizures, other kids fearfully avoided him, and my hope for his social acceptance died. Every tangible refuge was gone . . . or so I thought.

As a Bible teacher and small group leader, I knew that Scripture talked about refuge, but rather than seeking refuge in God, I looked for refuge in His ability to use "Plan B." A refuge, to me, was God providing something good to compensate for something bad. With each diagnosis, my focus shifted from the disappointing circumstance to the next compensation: *Surely, God will use Daniel's mind. Surely, God will use his social ability.* God, however, had a better refuge to offer.

Through the unfolding life of my firstborn, God tenderly exposed my unreliable refuges and forced me to examine my heart. Where did I seek refuge? What was true refuge anyway? Could a reliable refuge even be found? Weary of refuges that changed or failed, I set out to discover how the Scriptures would answer those questions.

What I found in the Bible surprised me. I expected refuge to look like perennial gardens, quiet waters, and lakeside retreats. I thought it would provide a place of quiet safety where I could flee the pressures and heartaches of everyday life. Biblical refuge, I learned, was something quite different. Most "refuge" passages contained active battle images, not the quiet, hiding-place scenes I expected. Biblical refuge wasn't escape from reality nor was it positive thinking. What was it then?

The fortress passages I studied reminded me of fortified castles I visited while temporarily living in Europe in 1996. I clearly remember the security I felt standing behind the castle walls; though I felt hardship and warfare, I simultaneously sensed provision and peace. As I studied the history of these keeps, I learned that these castles were military strongholds built for defense. Like biblical fortresses, they provided protection during siege but were also places of ordinary life. Military barracks, intricate defense systems, civilian living quarters, gardens, kitchens, stables, infirmaries, reception halls, chapels, the lord's chambers—these existed side-by-side within the fortress. People lived and worked, loved and laughed, bled and died, all within the castle walls. Everyday life, and all it included, occurred in a place of refuge.

As I thought about these fortresses and recalled that God is portrayed as a fortress in Scripture, my understanding of refuge in Him began to change. Refuge wasn't silver linings or escape *from* life; refuge occurred *in the midst of* life. How? That's what this book is about.

Our Mighty Fortress addresses the mistaken idea that refuge in God means escape from the hardships of this world. It presupposes that true, biblical refuge is possible amid the pace, problems, and pains of everyday life.

We tend to think of refuge as circumstantial comfort, escape from difficulty, or relief from everyday responsibilities and normal routine. Biblical refuge, however, is not a physical place to which we flee, an immunity or protection from hardship, or a ceasing of pressure and activity. It is not something we take from God or that God gives to us, as in giving or receiving a gift; it is, rather, an experience of the very presence of God. *True, biblical refuge is an internal experience of God that, regardless of circumstance, provides continual rest for the soul.*

Misunderstanding refuge was exactly my problem during the heartbreaking years of Daniel's diagnoses. Through all we endured, God remained a distant figure to me. While I hoped He would provide, God Himself remained a stranger. Yes, Christ was my Savior and Lord. I knew the basic doctrines of the faith. I tried to please God, and regularly studied His Word. But I missed the fact that God's primary desire for me was relationship with Him (Matthew 22:37–38). The Bible, I realized, wasn't just a set of facts and principles; it was God's revelation of Himself (John 1:1). Truth was a *Person* (John 14:6), and biblical refuge was found in that Person.

I began to prayerfully study God's Word, not for theological knowledge or situational guidance, but simply to know Him. As I grew in knowing the God of the Bible and began to trust Him, my perspective changed. I began viewing *all* of my circumstances, both good and bad, through the unchanging lens of God's loving character. I discovered refuge in the Person of God.

What is God's refuge like? How do we experience it? This book attempts to answer these and other questions as it guides us on a journey through the Fortress of God.

To help us visualize our journey, this book is structured around the image of a medieval fortified castle (see diagram on pages 18–19). The castle, as a whole, represents refuge in God. To experience His refuge, we must first enter the Fortress. (We will learn how to do this in chapters 1 and 2). Upon entrance, we discover that refuge in God includes far more than crossing the drawbridge or passing the gate. The remaining chapters will lead us through the castle's subsequent rooms and structures, each providing a different, progressively more intimate, aspect of refuge.

Each chapter contains exercises and questions designed to

deepen the refuge experience. While completion of these exercises isn't necessary to experiencing refuge, they will aid us in our journey. If we take time to prayerfully interact with what is provided, we may find ourselves experiencing God in ways we never have before.

Before we begin, please understand two things. First, this is not a book *about* refuge; it is a book designed to *foster* refuge. Refuge in God isn't found in these pages; it is found in the God described in these pages. It isn't found in a classroom, but in the closet of prayer. It isn't found in this study, but in silence before Him. It isn't found in your head, but in your heart's response to Him. The experience of refuge comes from God alone as you interact with Him.

Second, though I have traveled this path for many years, I am a fellow sojourner. Though I've experienced something of God's refuge, I've also learned that there are hidden rooms and passages yet to be explored! Since God is truly "unsearchable" (Romans 11:33), I will continue this journey for the rest of my natural life.

Come now. Join me on a journey through the Mighty Fortress of God. I trust that as God has been my refuge over the past decade of Daniel's life, He will do the same for you. My prayer is that, as we seek His refuge, God will make Himself known to us and provide lasting rest for our souls.

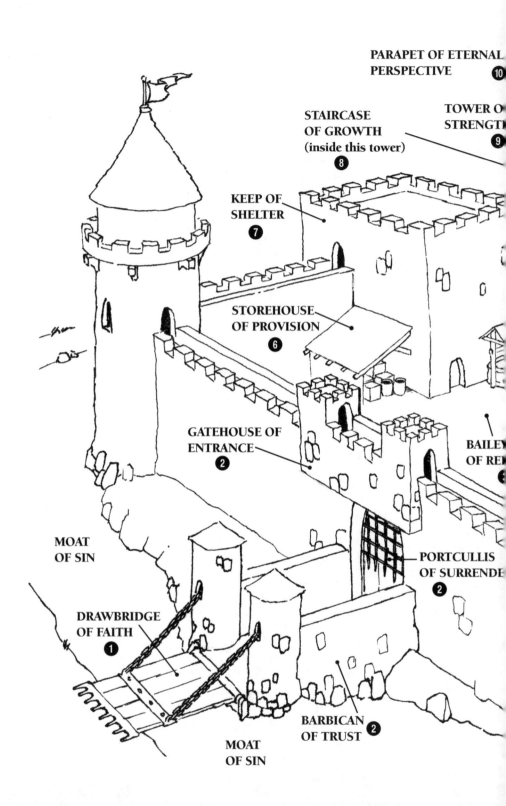

PARAPET OF ETERNAL
PERSPECTIVE   ❿

TOWER O
STRENGT
❾

STAIRCASE
OF GROWTH
(inside this tower)
❽

KEEP OF
SHELTER
❼

STOREHOUSE
OF PROVISION
❻

GATEHOUSE OF
ENTRANCE
❷

BAILE
OF RE

MOAT
OF SIN

PORTCULLIS
OF SURRENDE
❷

DRAWBRIDGE
OF FAITH
❶

BARBICAN
OF TRUST   ❷

MOAT
OF SIN

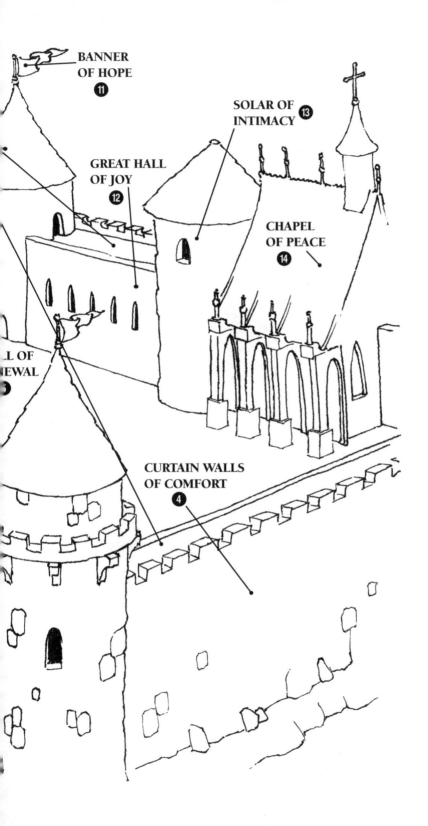

BANNER
OF HOPE
11

SOLAR OF
INTIMACY **13**

GREAT HALL
OF JOY
12

CHAPEL
OF PEACE
14

L OF
EWAL

CURTAIN WALLS
OF COMFORT
4

PART ONE

The Outer Regions

—⊱⋇⊰—

*You have looked for me in the outside world of emotions, yet all
the while I have been waiting inside for you. Meet Me now in
the inner chamber of your spirit, for I am there.*

—⊱⋇⊰—

L. B. COWMAN
Streams in the Desert (updated edition)

You are about to embark on a journey, an inward sojourn of the soul through the Mighty Fortress of God. Unlike outward journeys, the success of this journey doesn't depend on your planning, your knowledge, your resources, or your ability. It ultimately doesn't depend on you at all. The success of this pilgrimage depends upon the Person within these castle walls.

The Lord of the Fortress waits for you there. Won't you join Him?

1

GOD'S OPEN ARMS:
The Drawbridge of Faith

The gate of salvation is set open to all. There is nothing else to hinder us from entering, but our own unbelief.

JOHN CALVIN
The Acts of the Apostles, vol. 1

"I am the gate; whoever enters through me will be saved."

JESUS
John 10:9

-+->-<+-

Therefore, since we have been justified through faith, we have peace with God through our Lord Jesus Christ, through whom we have gained access by faith.

—ROMANS 5:1–2A

As my sister and I loaded suitcases, kids, and travel munchies into the car to begin our five-day "moms and kids only" weekend away, I thought: *South Carolina, here we come!* After several demanding months of ministry, I looked forward to a time of rest and relaxation. Leaving Wednesday afternoon, we drove partway through the night, slept at a Comfort Inn off I-95, and completed our trip the next morning. We arrived in Hilton Head at lunchtime, and were on the beach by two o'clock that afternoon.

It was a glorious Easter weekend in April: eighty-five degrees, cool ocean breeze, brilliant warm sun, and cloudless blue sky. Exhausted from the long drive, I was ready to snuggle in for a nap while our five kids (ranging in ages from nine to seventeen) bodysurfed in the gentle, rolling waves.

As I closed my eyes for much-needed rest, something in me said, *Don't sleep, Joan. Keep your eye on Dan.* I was tired and craved sleep, but my inner prompting kept nagging, *Keep watching Daniel.* So I slouched in my beach chair, kept my eyes open, and watched my seventeen-year-old firstborn.

Not ten minutes into my vigil, I saw Dan turn around and swim back toward the beach. Coming in from deeper waters, he crossed a submerged sandbar, waded slowly through waves, and stopped twenty yards off shore. Looking right at me, he screamed, "MOM, HELP!" and then collapsed into the water. He was having a full-blown seizure (something he hadn't had since his seizure disorder had been brought under control two years ago).

I shot out of my chair, sprinting across the beach and into

the waves. My fourteen-year-old daughter, Sarah, got to Dan first and pulled his head out of the calf-deep tide. By the time I got there, he was actively convulsing. I rolled Dan onto his side, cradled his head (to keep him from breathing water into his lungs), and started counting. (I didn't have a watch on, but long ago learned to time the different phases of Dan's seizures. Counting was my means of timing.) His convulsive phase lasted only about a minute this time.

As I held my son's head in my lap, I was deeply reminded of the certainty of God's refuge. Here on an island in South Carolina, I knew God was with us. He cradled my heart as surely as I cradled Dan's head. His cradling protected me from swirling emotions every bit as much as my cradling protected Daniel from swirling tides. In that moment, God was my refuge.

Fifteen years ago, that would not have been the case. I would not have sought, nor experienced, God's refuge the way I did in the ocean that day. Why? Because I didn't know how. In the early years of Daniel's life, I didn't really know what refuge was or how to experience it.

REFUGE DEFINED

Refuge, as we noted in the introduction, is found in the presence of God within us. *It is an internal experience of God that provides continual rest for the soul.*

We see this kind of experience when the Old Testament figure David, while under great duress, still managed to "lie down and sleep in peace" (Psalm 4:8). We see it when Stephen, even as he was stoned to death, looked to heaven with hope and joy (Acts 7:54–60). We see it in the quiet trust of a Galilean teen who, though still a virgin, was told she would give birth to the Son of God (Luke 1:26–38). These biblical men and women experienced refuge in God in the midst of tough circumstances. And though their circumstances didn't change, they found rest for their souls. Refuge, for them, wasn't an external solving of their problems; it was an internal experience of God. It is no less so for us.

Biblical refuge is internal. Because it is internal, we can seek refuge anytime, anyplace, and in any situation, even on South Carolina beaches. The question is: How? How do we find refuge in God in the heat of the moment or in the hubbub of life? The key to experiencing refuge is learning to make God our refuge.

Nineteenth-century preacher and evangelist Charles Spurgeon, in his classic commentary on the Psalms, wrote, "It is but poor comfort to say 'the Lord is a refuge,' but to say he is *my* refuge is the essence of consolation."[1] This is our trouble. We know in some abstract sense that God is a refuge. We rightly encourage one another to take refuge in God. We quote Scripture saying, "God is our refuge and strength, an ever-present help in trouble" (Psalm 46:1). We remind ourselves that God is a mighty fortress to which we can flee. And while we know these truths in our heads, we have difficulty applying them to our hearts. For us, God is simply a refuge. How do we make Him our refuge?

For several summers, when our children were young, we vacationed with my husband's family in Ocean City, New Jersey. Toward the end of our long drive, we eagerly scanned the horizon to see who could spot Great Egg Harbor first. It was a welcome site, signaling the end of our six-hour journey.

On one such trip, we spied the harbor and began to anticipate the toe-warming sand and refreshing sea breeze. Instead of our usual ten-minute drive over the bridge, across town, and to the beach, however, we found ourselves sweltering in standstill traffic.

What blocked our access to the island? Unknown to us, a mile ahead, the harbor's drawbridge had been raised to make way for passing ships. With the drawbridge up, we had no way to cross the harbor. We were stuck on the opposite shore.

When God is only *a* refuge, He seems like Ocean City as viewed from the other side of the harbor that day: far away and inaccessible. To make God *our* refuge, we must cross the Drawbridge of Faith. The joy for us, fellow traveler, is that the Drawbridge is always down. God stands ready to welcome us, if only we will come.

CROSSING THE DRAWBRIDGE OF FAITH

We begin our journey by crossing the Drawbridge. Why do we need a drawbridge? A moat of sin stands in our way. Just as Great

Egg Harbor blocked our family's access to Ocean City, so sin bars every person's access to God.

When I was a little girl, I loved to go fishing. To go fishing, you need bait. On muggy summer nights after a steady rain, I'd be outside on my hands and knees with a flashlight in my mouth, hunting for nightcrawlers (big, fat worms). The idea was to spot a worm beneath the grass, pounce on it with your fingers, then slowly and gently pull the nightcrawler out of its hole without breaking it. I learned this technique from my mother, who, good sport that she is, was out there on her hands and knees with me catching worms. On one particularly fruitful night, we must have caught more than fifty of them.

"Go show your Aunt Mel," my mother urged me after we surveyed our catch. I was proud of our accomplishment, so with muddy hands holding a slimy, writhing mass of living bait, I ran to our cottage door and knocked with my foot. My visiting aunt came to the door and stood at the screen.

"What do you have there?" she probed. While still standing outside, I held the squirming ball of worms right up to her face as she looked through the screen door.

"Oh, no you don't," she said, shaking her head. "You can't come in. You can't bring *those* in here!"

Sin is like the muddy mass of worms I carried to the cottage door; it keeps us from entering God's house. God created us for relationship with Himself, but we rejected Him. Isaiah 53:6 tells us, "We all, like sheep, have gone astray, each of us has turned to his own way." We have lived apart from God. We've made our own kingdoms, been our own kings, ruled our own lives, and sought our own answers. This living independent of God is what the Bible calls sin, and it covers us from head to toe.

God, however, is perfectly pure, without sin. Because He is sinless, He cannot allow sin into His presence. Though God longs for us to enter the Fortress, the muddiness of our sin keeps us on the moat's far side.

The good news is that He doesn't leave us there. God, the true King and Lord of the Fortress, loves us passionately and desires a relationship with us. He wants us to enter His refuge, but knows we are covered with sin. In mercy, He has set in place a drawbridge.

That drawbridge is a Person.

- "You see, at just the right time, when we were still powerless, Christ died for the ungodly" (Romans 5:6).
- "The Lord Jesus Christ . . . gave himself for our sins to rescue us . . . according to the will of our God and Father" (Galatians 1:3–4).
- "But now a righteousness from God . . . has been made known. . . . This righteousness from God comes through faith in Jesus Christ to all who believe" (Romans 3:21–22).

Because God loves us so much, He sent His Son, Jesus, to solve the sin problem (John 3:16). Jesus lived a pure and sinless life. He had a perfect record, a clean slate, if you will. Jesus wasn't sinful like us; He was righteous. He could stand in God's presence.

God solves our sin problem by offering Christ's righteousness to cover our sinfulness. Jesus rescues us by giving us His perfect record while taking the punishment our sins deserved. Jesus is the drawbridge that spans our moat of sin. Faith in Him is what enables us to cross.

FAITH TO CROSS THE MOAT

What does it mean to have faith in Jesus? Imagine standing on the edge of the moat. You want so much to cross the moat and enter the Fortress, but you realize there is nothing you can do to get yourself there. The boat of good works has no oars. It leaks and would sink before you arrived. The moat is infested with crocodiles that devour all who try to swim. The rope of religiosity isn't long enough to span the distance. And though the drawbridge is down, a padlocked chain bars your way.

You are helpless. There is only one thing left to do: Call out to the Lord of the Fortress.

So you cry out to Him. "Lord, I'm helpless. I can't cross this moat of sin. I need You and want to enter Your Fortress. Please, have mercy on me."

You look down, and there, materializing in your hand, is a brass key marked with only one word: *Faith*. As you turn it over, it solidifies in your hand. You feel its weight and watch it glisten in the sun. Admiring the key, however, won't get you across. You have to use it.

You insert the key into the padlock, and the chain spanning the Drawbridge entrance disappears. You look at the Drawbridge and wonder, *Is it really sufficient to carry me?* Finally you decide, *Yes, it will,* and with that decision you entrust your full weight to the sufficiency of the Drawbridge. You take a step forward and, the next thing you know, an unseen hand carries you across the Drawbridge to the Fortress entrance.

You feel different, maybe lighter somehow. You look down and realize that, in crossing the Drawbridge, your clothes changed. Pure white robes of righteousness have replaced the sin-stained, muddy garments you wore on the opposite shore! Your sin is gone! You can stand in the presence of God.

Faith is simply a heartfelt cry to God that realizes its helplessness, believes Jesus is who He claimed to be, accepts His invitation, and trusts Him to provide access to God. If you've sincerely recognized your need to be rescued, if you've asked Jesus to be your Savior and Lord, and if you believe that He lived, died, and rose again to reconcile you to God, you've crossed the Drawbridge. Your refuge journey has begun.

If, however, you have never truly accepted God's gift of righteousness in Jesus Christ, you cannot experience His refuge. This, dear reader, is why we must begin here. Without faith, you are still on your own; you have no access to God's Fortress. To experience His refuge, you must first cross the Drawbridge of Faith. If you have never done so, you can now by admitting your need, crying out to God, and believing that Jesus alone is your rescue.

If you've crossed the Drawbridge of Faith for the very first time, welcome to the family of God! If you're already a Christian, but seek refuge, know this: God's arms are waiting; His invitation to refuge stands. You're already over the Drawbridge and well on your way. But read on, for we must pass through the Gatehouse.

-<+- PUTTING IT INTO PRACTICE -+>-

Take a moment and ask God to give you the faith you need to enter His Fortress. If you have never crossed the Drawbridge of Faith, this prayer may help you start your journey:

Dear God,
I need refuge and want to enter a relationship with You, but I've created a moat between us by living my own way. I am muddy with sin and I'm helpless to make myself clean enough to stand in Your sinless presence. Have mercy on me, O God. Forgive me.

Thank You for Jesus. Thank You for sending Him to span the moat of my sin. I believe that He alone makes my relationship with You possible, that He is the only way into Your Fortress. I turn away from my sinful way of living and accept Jesus' righteousness. Thank You for saving me through Him. I ask Jesus to be my Savior and Lord and surrender my life to You now.

If you have prayed this prayer to cross the moat, you have found the true refuge. You are ready to begin the journey. Congratulations! (For more information and materials on beginning your life with God and His Son Jesus, please contact the publisher at the address shown on the final page of this book.)

Questions for Reflection

1. What drove you to seek refuge in God?

2. When you think of God, is He merely a refuge or is He your refuge?

3. When did you first cross over the Drawbridge of Faith? Describe your experience.

4. Read Ephesians 2:4–9. What does this passage mean to you?

5. What have you learned about God in this chapter?

Note

1. Charles Haddon Spurgeon, *The Treasury of David, vol. 2, part 1* (McLean, Va.: MacDonald, n.d.), 89.

2
OUR YIELDED HANDS:
The Gatehouse of Entrance

God calls upon us to yield our wills up unto Him, that He may take the control of them, and may work in us to will and to do of His good pleasure. If we will obey this call . . . He will take possession of our surrendered wills and will begin at once to work in us.

HANNAH WHITALL SMITH
The Christian's Secret of a Happy Life

"Yield your hearts to the LORD, the God of Israel"

JOSHUA
Joshua 24:23

⊹⊱⊰⊹

He who dwells in the shelter of the Most High
will rest in the shadow of the Almighty.
I will say of the LORD, "He is my refuge and my
fortress, my God, in whom I trust."

—PSALM 91:1–2

Truth be told, I'm not a very good traveler. Don't get me wrong; I enjoy going places and seeing different parts of the world. Foreign cultures fascinate me, and I even briefly lived overseas. The destination part of travel isn't what I find disagreeable; it's the process of getting there. Traveling makes me feel incompetent (especially when the airline changes its passenger guidelines). Traveling puts me in unfamiliar territory (then I have to learn a bunch of new rules). Traveling disrupts my regular routine and stretches me way beyond my comfort zone. (I do wish I was more elastic.) But the worst part of traveling for me is that I'm not in control.

Three months ago, after boarding a plane in Brussels, Belgium, I sat on that plane for *fifteen* consecutive hours. (Boy, was I glad I brought drinking water along.) Just two weeks later, we had a *twenty-four*-hour flight delay. (At least the airline bused us to a hotel.) Earlier this year, when boarding a cruise ship bound for Alaska, the cruise line's entire computer system crashed and they had to register thousands of embarking guests by hand. The frustrating thing about all of these scenarios was that I couldn't control what was happening. I had to surrender my agenda, go along for the ride, and trust those in charge.

Whenever I travel, I give up the right to control all the details. I entrust myself to the competencies of those running the show. With every journey I take, I put myself into someone else's hands. The journey into our Mighty Fortress is no different.

ARRIVING AT THE GATEHOUSE OF ENTRANCE

The Drawbridge of Faith brought us to the Gatehouse of Entrance. This is our only way into the Fortress of God. If you look to your left and right, you'll notice that we've come to a narrow-walled passage. Behind us is the Drawbridge; up ahead waits a heavy iron grill. In a medieval fortress, guards would have stood watch here, but guards aren't necessary in this Fortress. The only thing keeping us from entering the Fortress is this outer corridor, called a *barbican,* and the grate up ahead, called a *portcullis.* To enter the Fortress we must be willing to take this path through the Barbican of Trust and the Portcullis of Surrender. Trust and surrender are the only way in.

CROSSING THE BARBICAN OF TRUST

What is trust? Several years ago, our doctor called to tell us that traditional medicine could do nothing more for our youngest son, Jonathan's, chronic intestinal disorder. I desperately needed refuge and faced a choice. I could listen to the doubts nagging at my heart—*this is out of control; God must not love us; I can't handle this*—or I could choose to trust God and surrender our circumstances to Him. As I wrestled with the implications of our doctor's words, I ignored my feelings and chose to believe what God said—*He is always in control; He loves us more than we know; His grace is sufficient to equip us.* In other words, I trusted God.

Trust is assured, confident reliance on who God is and what He says. It is taking God at His word, and being certain that He will keep His word. Fourteenth century English mystic Lady Julian of Norwich noted that "what delights [God] most, is when we pray simply trusting in his goodness, holding on to him, relying upon his grace, with true understanding, rather than if we made all the means that [we] can think. Even when we summon all such skills, we are bound to fall short: all we need do is trust in God's own goodness, for this will never fail us."[1] When we are certain of God, and depend on that certainty, we trust God.

Best-selling author Jerry Bridges wrote in his classic, *Trusting God,* "Trust is not a passive state of mind. It is a vigorous act of the soul by which we choose to lay hold on the promises of God and cling to them despite the adversity that at times seeks to overwhelm us."[2]

Trust, at its most basic level, is a conscious choice, and it's a choice made regardless of circumstance. King David wrote, "Trust in [God] at *all* times" (Psalm 62:8; emphasis added). Whatever our adversity or heartache, whatever drives us to seek refuge, we can choose to trust God. It is a deliberate act of the will.

That is exactly what I did while holding Daniel's head out of the water in Hilton Head that Easter weekend. In the middle of assaulting thoughts and emotions, I made the deliberate choice to believe that God was in control, that He loved us, and that He had some purpose for what was happening. I willed myself to trust Him, and in so doing experienced His refuge.

Don't assume, however, that because trust is a choice, it will be easy to make that choice. Trust is rarely easy. It sometimes goes against every fiber of our being.

THE DIFFICULTY OF TRUST

Years ago, I led rock-climbing trips for a Christian camp in southwestern Pennsylvania. The campers were always eager to try their hand at ascending a rock face, and did so with abandon. The climbing part was fun. Rappelling—going down after the climb—was challenging, however, especially for the boys.

After each climber completed his ascent, he topped out, stepped away from the cliff's edge, and unclipped his safety harness from the climbing safety line. Then he walked, maybe fifty yards, down a wooded path along the precipice to the rappel site. This stroll along the rock's edge gave each climber the opportunity to see just how high he'd climbed, and just how far away he was from the ground below. It also gave him plenty of time to think about how he was going to get down. By the time the boys got to me at the top of the rappel, they were pretty nervous.

When a climber reached the rappel site, I immediately clipped a secured safety rope (called a belay line) to his seat harness. Once attached to the line, the climber yelled, "On belay!" (meaning "secured to the belay line"). I responded, "Belay on!" Next, he moved to the cliff's edge and called, "Rappelling" (meaning "ready to descend"), to which I answered, "Rappel on." Now all he had to do was step over the edge backward, while I held his life in my belaying hands.

The last thing a fourteen-year-old, testosterone-driven male wants to do is admit fear or dependency. But there is nothing like stepping backward into a one hundred-fifty-foot chasm to make him realize how dependent he really is. When each young man took that backward step off the cliff, he had to trust me and my ability as a belayer over every instinct that screamed in protest.

I'll tell you, time after time it was the macho, self-assured, cocky "I can do anything" teen who withered in tears at the cliff's edge. He couldn't rely on himself anymore; he had to trust someone else for his safety. Trusting someone other than oneself went against every grain of adolescent bravado.

The meek teen, on the other hand, the quiet guy or girl who trusted less in self and was learning to depend on others, stepped over with confidence. Each knew his limitations and trusted me without question.

I had to smile as these youths rappelled; rappelling was the great equalizer in the competitive world of teenage boys. Interestingly enough, every camper who made it to the bottom of the rappel, no matter how difficult (or easy) it was for him to first step off the cliff, couldn't wait to get back up and do it again. With each decision to trust, it grew easier to trust the next time.

Trusting God may be a similar experience for us. When we first make the choice to trust God, our inner resources may scream in protest. The choice to trust Him when it makes no sense to do so will take every ounce of courage we have. But each time we make the deliberate, willful choice to trust God, we discover a paradox of trust: By choosing to trust God, we experience His refuge; and the more we experience His refuge, the easier it is to trust.

When we choose to trust God, we step across the Barbican. Won't you take the first step and trust Him now?

Trust alone, however, isn't enough to access the Fortress. We must also pass through the Portcullis of Surrender.

PASSING THROUGH THE PORTCULLIS OF SURRENDER

Moving beyond the heavy iron grating of a castle—the portcullis —is not easy, and at times surrender seems the same way. Who wants to give up control? Actually, though, surrender is nothing more than yielding yourself, your possessions, and your circumstances to someone else (in this case, God). It is giving up on your own resources and entrusting yourself to the power of another. When that Person is altogether trustworthy, this is easy to do.

When I surrendered Jonathan's health situation to God, I gave up my need to be in control, stopped relying on my resources, and offered my circumstances to the One I knew to be faithful and good; I put the situation in His hands, and let go.

My surrender was nothing compared to that of the Old Testament patriarch Abraham. He also faced a situation that required surrender, though the potential consequences of his yielding were far greater than mine. God promised Abraham a son through Sarah (Genesis 18:10), though both were old and Sarah was barren. Their son would be heir to God's promise that Abraham's descendants would outnumber the stars (Genesis 15:4–5). God fulfilled His promise in Isaac (Genesis 21:1–3), but, as God often does, He called upon Abraham to give up what was most precious to him. God commanded Abraham to sacrifice Isaac—his only son by Sarah, the one whom he loved (Genesis 22:2), the heir of the promise.

I can't imagine fully what Abraham thought as he climbed the hill with his soon-to-be-sacrificed son. The Bible tells us he thought God would provide (Genesis 22:8). But when it came time for the sacrifice, no lamb was in sight. Abraham would have to kill his son. Abraham picked up his knife, and when he raised his knife to sacrifice Isaac, he surrendered not only his hopes and dreams for young Isaac's life, but his own future and progeny as well. Abraham put it all in God's hands, and moved his own hand to slay his son.

It was then that God revealed the ram (Genesis 22:10–13), and Abraham experienced God's provision as never before.

God calls us to surrender our circumstances, even when it makes no sense to do so. We're called to give Him the things we love most, even when we can't see His plan. Can you see how critical trust is to surrender? That is why we had to pass through the Barbican of Trust before coming here. If we don't trust God, we won't surrender to Him. The two go hand in hand.

Scripture instructs us to "trust in the LORD with all your heart and lean not on your own understanding" (Proverbs 3:5). When we trust God, we can give up our understanding and relinquish control to the only one who is in control. As Abraham did in the mountains of Moriah, so we, too, can surrender to Him.

TRUST AND SURRENDER: ONLY THE BEGINNING

Trust and surrender move us through the Barbican, under the Portcullis, and into the Fortress of God. While they provide access to the Fortress, lasting refuge is found beyond the Gatehouse within the castle walls. Though we've entered the Fortress, our refuge journey has only begun.

Before we continue, take heed: Faith, trust, and surrender will not end our pain or our problems. Our heartaches remain and our trials continue. We learn, however, that they drive us to the deeper refuge found further inside the Fortress. Join me as we step into the first regions of God's Fortress refuge. It is there that we deepen our experience of Him.

-<- PUTTING IT INTO PRACTICE ->-

Many things can bar our paths through the Gatehouse: busyness, worry, inattention to God's Word, unbelief, and distraction by false comforts (TV, novels, food, possessions, etc.), among others. The primary barrier, however, is misplaced trust. When I need refuge, instead of trusting God, I'm tempted to trust in:

- Intellect: If I can make sense of this, I'll be OK.
- Understanding: If I know why, I'll find comfort.
- Organizational skills: My plan can solve this problem.
- Experience: This worked before, so it will surely work again.
- Information: The more I know, the more I'm in control.
- Professionals (doctors, lawyers, etc.): They can solve my problem.
- Friends or family: Their love and support will make me feel better.

Although none of these is inherently bad, trusting these instead of God bars our access to His refuge. In which Gatehouse barrier listed above are you most tempted to trust? You may have more than one. Take a moment to identify them. Then pray and ask God to help you stop trusting in each false refuge. Ask Him to help you trust fully and solely in Him.

Questions for Reflection

1. Do you believe that God is trustworthy? Why or why not?

2. How is trust related to surrender?

3. Author and missionary L. B. Cowman, in her classic devotional *Streams in the Desert,* wrote, "It is never too late for God to deal triumphantly with . . . things if they are brought to Him in complete surrender and trust."[3] What connection do you see between our trust, surrender, and God's work in our lives?

4. Read Proverbs 3:5–6. What do you think it means to "trust in the LORD with all your heart" and "lean not on your understanding?"

5. In what ways are trust and surrender related to experiencing refuge in God?

Notes

1. Julian of Norwich, *Revelation of Love,* ed. and trans. John Skinner (New York: Doubleday, 1996), 6–7.
2. Jerry Bridges, *Trusting God* (Colorado Springs: NavPress, 1988), 200.
3. L. B. Cowman, *Streams in the Desert,* ed. James Reimann, updated edition (Grand Rapids: Zondervan, 1997), November 22, 436.

3

IT'S GOOD TO BE HOME:
The Bailey of Relief

For too long we have been in a far country: a country of noise and hurry and crowds, a country of climb and push and shove, a country of frustration and fear and intimidation. And God welcomes us home: home to serenity and peace and joy, . . . home to intimacy and acceptance and affirmation. We do not need to be shy. He invites us.

RICHARD FOSTER
Prayer

⇥⟩⟨⟨

God is just: He will . . . give relief to you who are troubled.

—2 THESSALONIANS 1:6–7

For you did not receive a spirit that makes you a slave again to fear, but you received the Spirit of sonship. And by him we cry, "Abba, Father." The Spirit himself testifies with our spirit that we are God's children.

—ROMANS 8:15–16

Ahh, you made it! In faith, trust, and surrender, you passed through the Gatehouse, and now you're here. Welcome to the Fortress where we find our refuge in God.

What is it like when you first enter a fortress? You step into the bailey: a wide grassy expanse within the castle walls. You smell the blacksmith's fire and hear his mallet clang. The musty smell of damp hay assaults your smoke-filled nose. You simultaneously hear horses neighing, chickens squawking, children giggling, and vendors bartering. It's market day, and the bailey echoes with endless noise and nagging distractions. Yet, you stand behind your father's walls. You've come home.

I remember the first time I really understood what it meant to find my home with God. My husband and I were living in France during a temporary three-month business relocation. We had a problem with our mail, and I'd gone to the post office to resolve the matter. Though my language skills were adequate for basic dialogue, I couldn't seem to make the postmaster understand my broken French. Feeling isolated, frustrated, and humiliated by my inability to communicate, I left quickly without solving the problem.

As I pushed through the vendor-filled streets, all I could think of was how alone and misunderstood I felt. I was the literal American in Paris, out of place, lonely, and I wanted to go home. There was one big problem: Home, my geographical home, was thousands of miles away on the other side of the Atlantic.

Back at the apartment, as I muddled through my jumbled emotions, it dawned on me that I wasn't just a foreigner in Europe; as a Christian, I was a foreigner in this world (Psalm 119:19). God seemed to help me realize that I wasn't homesick for a physical place or geographic location; I really hungered for acceptance, belonging, and love. Even in Pennsylvania, I'd known that longing.

HOME: A PLACE OF LOVE

You see, home, in its truest sense, is a place of being known, understood, accepted, and loved. It's a place of belonging. God gently reminded me that I had all this, and more, with Him.

Did you know that when you entered the Mighty Fortress of God you came home? Yes, *home!* When you crossed the Drawbridge of Faith, you became a child of God, a joint heir with Christ (see Romans 8:16–17). We "are no longer foreigners and aliens, but fellow citizens with God's people and members of God's household" (Ephesians 2:19). This fortress refuge is our home. When God is our refuge, we can enjoy His love, acceptance, and tender welcome anytime, in anyplace, in any circumstance. What sweet relief we find in coming home to Him!

WHAT IS RELIEF?

Relief is simply that part of God's refuge where we experience the lightening of our load. It is a lessening of the distress or pain we carry. It is the rest that comes not from outwardly stopping our activity or doing restful things but in inwardly ceasing to carry the weight of our concerns alone. At the Bailey of Relief we find a welcome, green courtyard amid the busyness around us. Here God shoulders our burdens and eases our cares.

Have you ever been backpacking? Before we had children, my husband and I enjoyed backpacking together. One of our weekend excursions brought us to a loop on the Black Forest Trail near Williamsport, Pennsylvania. This moderately difficult trail winds through heavy woodland, steep ravines, and scenic vistas of Pine Creek Gorge. On this particular trip, I hurt my knee (we later discovered that I'd shredded some cartilage), and hiking hills became excruciating. My thirty-pound pack seemed to grow heavier with each new step, and while limping along a precipice, I feared I might fall. Halfway up the steep wooded incline, I could go no farther. My husband, Don, bless his heart, had to hike to the top of the ravine, leave his pack, climb back down, pick up my pack, and carry it to the summit for me.

The burdens we carry in life can sometimes feel like my pack did on that painful journey. We bend under our burdens, afraid we might fall, or our burdens become too difficult to bear. The good news is that God has not abandoned us to carry our burdens alone. Listen to what Scripture says:

"Come to me, all you who are weary and burdened, and I will give you rest. Take my yoke upon you and learn from me, for I am gentle and humble in heart, and you will find rest for your souls. For my yoke is easy and my burden is light." (Matthew 11:28–30)

The Lord upholds all those who fall and lifts up all who are bowed down. (Psalm 145:14)

A bruised reed he will not break, and a smoldering wick he will not snuff out. (Isaiah 42:3)

God promises rest to the weary. He promises to lift us when we're bowed down. He won't allow us to break under the weight of our cares. Relief comes when we allow God to carry us through our trials. It comes when we give our burdens to Him.

HOW DO WE GIVE OUR BURDENS TO GOD?

How do we place our burdens on God? The real answer may surprise you: by being broken. Oscar Wilde once wrote, "How else but through a broken heart may Lord Christ enter in?"[1] To experience God's refuge and find relief from our burdens, we must come to the end of ourselves. We have to recognize our helplessness and realize that we cannot, nor were we designed to, bear our burdens alone.

Earlier this spring, our fourteen-year-old daughter wanted to invite a boy to her freshman formal. It wasn't that she wanted to go steady with this young man. It was just that she didn't want to be the "only" girl going without an escort. Don and I had earlier decided that Sarah would not "date" until she was sixteen, and then only if we felt she was sufficiently mature. When she did start dating we had two conditions: First, we had to know the boy or meet him ahead of time; second, he had to be a Christian.

The ninth-grade formal presented several challenges:

- Going one-on-one to a dance constituted a date (in our minds, not hers), and Sarah was only fourteen.
- We'd never met the boy.
- As far as we knew, he had not embraced the Christian faith.

Despite the fact that Sarah never gave us any reason to doubt her integrity or values, and despite the fact that she consistently displayed maturity, responsibility, and wisdom beyond her years, we could not allow her to attend the dance with this young man. She was understandably devastated when we told her she could not ask her friend to the dance.

It broke my heart to see her inconsolable tears! I knew that Sarah only wanted to be included, especially since she'd often felt left out because of stands she'd taken in school for her faith. Though I second-guessed our decision, we stood firm.

Our once warm, interactive daughter became cool and distant. As the formal approached, she withdrew even more, and I feared that our "no" may have pushed her away for good. The situation became a burden that weighed heavily on my heart. (You parents of teens can relate, I'm sure.)

I needed relief. How did I find it? I realized my inadequacy and gave Sarah completely to God. Her future and our relationship were in His hands, not mine. I'd done all I could do to responsibly parent my daughter and to reconcile our differences, but the outcome was beyond my control. In my mind, I visually lifted Sarah to God and asked Him to guard her from anger and bitterness. I prayed that He would protect her faith and our relationship. I envisioned Him taking her into His arms and carrying her close to His heart (Isaiah 40:11).

In that moment, I felt the weight of the decision lift from my shoulders. Did our circumstances change? No, but the weight was gone; I experienced relief.

Does relief from our burdens mean that our responsibilities end or our troubles cease? Not at all. In fact, we may carry some burdens for the rest of our natural lives (e.g., side effects of addiction, permanent disability, responsibility for children in or out of wedlock, chronic illness, financial hardship, etc.). In the freshman formal situation, we still had to parent our daughter regardless of the consequences or end result. Sarah could've allowed that single incident to harden her heart toward us and God. She might've become uncooperative and surly for months to come. Our relationship could've have been damaged for years. Thankfully, none of these happened. Our estrangement lasted only two weeks and then the relationship was restored, but I had to give Sarah continually to God during that time.

Relief meant that though our responsibility as parents continued and though we lived with the consequences, Don and I didn't bear the burden alone.

What burden do you carry? What load do you bear? Take a moment right now and envision yourself standing in the Bailey, struggling under the weight of your cares. Ask the Lord of the Fortress to uphold you. Recognize your weakness. Lift your burden to Him. When we relinquish our burdens and God gives us relief, we experience His refuge. We find rest when we allow God to carry us through.

The trouble-filled pack you've surrendered in the Bailey may not be the only load you carry. There are other less obvious burdens hiding deep within our souls.

GIVING HIM THE HIDDEN BURDENS

When we think about the things from which we need relief, we often think of life's external pressures and circumstances:

- family demands
- disharmony in the church
- health challenges
- financial worries

- work deadlines
- persecution in the world
- unexpected tragedy
- conflict with loved ones or colleagues

These are but a few (I'm sure you have others), and we willingly give these to Jesus. But we have other burdens that are not so easily relinquished. While hidden, they are heavier and can prove more debilitating than external cares and woes.

What are these burdens? They are the internal burdens of the heart. While these burdens come in many shapes and sizes (bitterness, jealousy, pride, worry, anxiety, etc.), perhaps the heaviest is what pastor and author A.W. Tozer describes in *The Pursuit of God*:

> The labor of self-love is a heavy one indeed. . . . The heart's fierce effort to protect itself from every slight . . . will never let the mind have rest. Continue this fight through the years and the burden will become intolerable. Yet [we carry] this burden continually, challenging every word spoken against [us], cringing under every criticism, smarting under each fancied slight, tossing sleepless if another is preferred."[2]

There is no rest in vigilant self-defense. Self-interest, self-centered love, self-protection—these are awful burdens to bear. There are others like them: perfectionism, people-pleasing, and approval-seeking.

The problem is these demand enormous amounts of energy to maintain. They require us to present an image to the world—a mask, if you will—behind which we hide. We hope no one sees underneath, because we think we won't be loved or accepted if known as we truly are. We fear being less than we hope to be.

That is the glory of coming home! God knows us inside and out; He sees beneath the mask. We don't have to fear Him discovering what lies beneath; He already knows! The truth is, we are far more sinful than we can possibly imagine, and God knows it all! Our relief comes in realizing that, though God knows the worst about us, He loves us still. The Cross forever settles the question of God's love for us. And because His love is unconditional, there is *nothing* we can do to make Him love us more, and *nothing* we can do to make Him love us less. His love is perfect and complete.

Fellow traveler, do you fear being known as you really are? Do you carry the burden of self-protection? Come; find relief in the Bailey. Leave this load here, too. God already knows your weakness and failings; He already knows your sin. Yet He loves you with an everlasting love (Jeremiah 31:3) and welcomes you home. Relief comes in realizing that God sees it all, yet delights in us still (Psalm 149:4).

-+- PUTTING IT INTO PRACTICE -+-

The busyness all around the Bailey of Relief can keep us from recognizing attitudes that rob us of relief in God's refuge. Which of the following attitudes most prevents you from finding relief from your burdens?

1. I don't really need help; I can carry this myself.
2. My problem is just too big for God to handle.
3. I really blew it this time; God won't want to help me.
4. God doesn't want to be bothered by my little problems.
5. Things are just fine; I don't really need God right now.
6. If I work hard enough, then God will give me relief.

Though we are tempted to believe these statements, each is a subtle lie that can rob us of relief in God's refuge. Which have you believed? Replace them with the following truths:

1. I do need help; apart from Christ I can do nothing (John 15:5).
2. Nothing is impossible with God (Matthew 19:26).
3. God is forgiving and abounding in love to all who call to Him (Psalm 86:5).
4. God longs to be gracious to me, and to show me compassion (Isaiah 30:18).
5. God is the source of all blessing in my life; I always need Him (1 Corinthians 4:7; Deuteronomy 8:17–18).
6. God's delight in me is based on grace, not my performance (Ephesians 2:8–9).

--⊁--≺--

Questions for Reflection

1. When was the first time you experienced God as your true home? Explain.

2. Would you say your relationship with God is characterized as "knowing about" Him or "knowing" Him? What can you do to better know Him?

3. From what circumstances do you most need relief? Take a moment now to offer each to God in prayer. Then let them go.

4. What internal burden(s) of the heart do you tend to carry most? What difference does knowing that God knows the worst about you, yet loves you still, make as you wrestle with that burden(s)?

5. Read Psalms 34:18 and 51:17. What encouragement do you find in these passages?

Notes

1. Oscar Wilde, *The Ballad of Reading Gaol,* part V, stanza 14, in *A Critical Edition of Major Works* (Oxford, England: Oxford University Press, 1989), 565.
2. A.W. Tozer, *The Pursuit of God* (Harrisburg, Pa.: Christian Publications, 1948), 112.

4

NEVER ALONE:
The Curtain Walls of Comfort

The knowledge that we are never alone calms the troubled sea of our lives and speaks peace to our souls.

A. W. TOZER
The Knowledge of the Holy

"I will never leave you nor forsake you."

GOD
Joshua 1:5

"And surely I am with you always."

JESUS
Matthew 28:20

When you were a child, did you ever try to lose your shadow? I tried it once, when I was about five years old. Playing on a sunny sidewalk in front of our suburban Washington, D.C., home, I tried again and again to outrun the dark figure that followed. No matter how many sudden stops and quick turns I made, my shadow wouldn't let go. It went with me everywhere.

Several years ago, I experienced a repeat of my childhood shadow experience. My husband and I took the kids to visit the Château de Fougères, an eleventh- to fifteenth-century border fortress near the Breton border in France. Upon entering this massive castle, I had the strange feeling that I couldn't "lose" its fortress walls. Everywhere I went within the fortress—shops, gardens, cafes, museums—the walls were always in view.

There was a reason for my feeling. A castle's curtain walls surrounded the fortress and connected its towers. They sheltered all affairs of castle life (buying, trading, eating, sleeping, working, playing, etc.). They were designed to provide protection and security even in the darkest, most remote corners of the fortress.

In a similar way God surrounds, shelters, and protects the affairs of our daily lives. Listen to what the psalmist says:

Where can I go from your Spirit? Where can I flee from your presence? If I go up to the heavens, you are there; if I make my bed in the depths, you are there. If I rise on the wings of the dawn, if I settle on the far side of the sea, even there your hand will guide me, your right hand will hold me fast. (Psalm 139:7–10)

God is always with us. When we seek His refuge, we find comfort in His presence. That doesn't mean that God magically appears as if He wasn't there before. It simply means that we become aware of Him. I began to understand this idea of God's comforting presence when I sat with my son late one evening.

COMFORT IN GOD'S PRESENCE

My younger son, Jonathan, had been wrestling with chronic stomach pain for months, and bedtimes were often the worst times for him. One night, his pain was particularly bad. As I tucked him into bed that night, he looked up at me and asked, "Mom, will you stay a little while?"

"Sure, Bud," I whispered and sat down next to him. His rapid breathing and occasional whimper told me he was hurting. I could do nothing to relieve him, so I tenderly brushed the hair out of his pain-filled eyes and waited with him for sleep to come. Soon enough the slow, deep rhythm of his breathing told me he was asleep.

Jonathan was in pain and found comfort in my presence. He asked me to stay and knew I was there. No words were necessary, no action. Just my presence was enough to calm and assure him. In the same way, God's presence calms and assures us.

What is your pain? What do you suffer? Perhaps you, too, have a sick child. Perhaps you bear the heartache of divorce. Yours may be the pain of loneliness, loss, false accusation, or betrayal. Or maybe you're weary of living in a sin-sick world. Whatever your circumstances, know this: When you enter the Mighty Fortress of God, He comforts you.

HOW DOES GOD'S PRESENCE COMFORT US?

God's presence can comfort us in many ways. Here are just three. *First, God's presence reminds us that we are not alone.* I hate it when my husband travels. I lie awake at night imagining every bump and rattle to be a serious threat or catastrophe waiting to happen. *What was that? Is someone breaking in? What if it's a murderer or rapist? Should I call the police?* It's rather silly, really. Here I am, a forty-something, level-headed woman, with three teenagers and two ferocious sounding Labrador retrievers, and yet I lie here in heart-thumping fear. Why? Because, I feel vulnerable. Don's presence reassures and comforts me. When he's away, I feel very much alone.

The truth, however, is that I am *never* alone, even when Don travels. Listen again to Scripture:

"Have I not commanded you? Be strong and courageous. Do not be terrified; do not be discouraged, for the LORD your God will be with you wherever you go." (Joshua 1:9)

"Do not be afraid, for I am with you." (Isaiah 43:5)

"'Never will I leave you; never will I forsake you.'" (Hebrews 13:5)

God is with us, and because He is, we are never alone. This sense of "un-aloneness" is the start of our experience of comfort in God's refuge.

Second, God's presence removes our fear. When Jonathan was nearly two, we discovered a great wooden playground with cones and spires, tower and tunnels, tire swings and twisty slides, all set in the shaded woodland of our community park. Wanting to explore every inch of this new wonderland, he toddled away from me, fearless, as long as I was in view.

Curious about what he'd do if he lost sight of me, I stepped behind a nearby oak. Hardly a moment passed when I heard his wail, "Mmoooooooommeeeeeeee!" Peeking from behind the massive trunk, I saw sheer terror in his eyes. His lower lip trembled. His eyes brimmed with tears. He was afraid because he thought he was alone.

When he found me, his eyes lit up, he giggled, and then ran to throw himself into my arms. He was no longer frightened because he knew I was there.

We are children of God (Romans 8:16); God loves us (John 3:16); nothing can separate us from His love (Romans 8:38–39); His love drives out fear (1 John 4:18), and He is always, always with us (Matthew 28:20). When facing uncharted waters, we can sail through them without fear. Why? Because we are secure in our Father's presence. God is with us, even when we can't see Him. And, though He may not remove our pain or change our circumstances, His presence calms our fear. This, too, is part of comfort.

Third, God's presence assures us that our suffering has purpose. What good can come from favoritism, hatred, jealousy, lies, and betrayal? What about famine, entrapment, false accusation, and arrest? Joseph could have asked all those questions. As a hated brother sold by his siblings into slavery, He remained a follower of God. This despite the following:

- Joseph's brothers plotted to kill him before finally agreeing to sell him as a slave (Genesis 37:20).

- Joseph's masters then sold him to another in Egypt (Genesis 39:1).

- His new master's wife falsely accused him of rape (Genesis 39:11–18).

- Joseph was thrown into prison (Genesis 39:19–20).

- While in prison, Joseph interpreted dreams for Pharaoh's imprisoned cupbearer. When released, the cupbearer failed to mention Joseph's kindness to the Pharoah, and Joseph languished in prison for two more years (Genesis 40:8–23).

Joseph's life was a nightmare by any standard. Can you imagine how his brothers' betrayals hurt him? Can you feel his angry indignation at being falsely accused? Can you empathize with the doubts, questions, and the feelings of abandonment he most certainly felt as he sat forgotten in prison? And yet, we're told repeatedly, "The Lord was with him" (Genesis 39:2–3, 21, 23). God didn't abandon Joseph. And not only did He not abandon him; God used Joseph's suffering for a greater good.

Several chapters later, we discover the reason for Joseph's hardships. (Read Genesis 40–50 for the rest of the story.) God had a good plan, one that included suffering. When Joseph finally revealed himself to his brothers, instead of seething hatred or bitterness, he greeted them with this: "Don't be afraid. . . . You intended to harm me, but God intended it for good to accomplish . . . the saving of many lives" (Genesis 50:19–20).

God used Joseph, and all he went through, to save His people during a time of severe famine. God had a purpose for Joseph's pain.

Are you suffering just now? Remember Joseph. Remember that God was with him, even in chains and a jail cell. Remember that God used all of it: the betrayal, the murderous plot, the false accusations, the bondage—*all* of it—to accomplish a plan far greater than Joseph could've imagined. There is a reason for our suffering, as God's presence reminds us, even when we can't see it or understand.

WE MISS GOD'S COMFORT BECAUSE . . .

So if God's presence is always there, why do we often feel so alone, afraid, and comfortless?

. . . WE FORGET HIS PRESENCE.

God is always there, yet unlike curtain walls surrounding a fortress, His presence can be overlooked. This lack of awareness, in part, is why we feel comfortless. Just like the harassed, helpless crowd living like sheep without a shepherd in Matthew 9:36, we live as though there is no God. We are a forgetful people.

A recent news item recounted how tragic forgetfulness can be. A young mother living in Texas ran some errands with her newborn strapped securely in the backseat of their van. The sleeping infant made no sound as she slumbered in her rear-facing car seat. Arriving home, the young woman parked in their sun-baked driveway and, distracted by the tasks at hand, forgot where her daughter was sleeping. Tragically, that day brought record-setting heat, and by the time the young mother remembered her child, the baby had died from heat exposure in the stifling, airless van.

How could a mother forget her sleeping child? I don't know. Certainly this woman loved her little girl and meant her no harm. My guess is that a single-minded focus on details obliterated any thought of her newborn. And so it is with us. We are so focused on our tasks and problems that we forget God.

. . . WE VIEW HIM WRONGLY.

Forgetfulness isn't the only thing that keeps us from experiencing God's comfort. We can remember He is there, but not know who He is. We view Him wrongly.

My sociology professor in college was a pastor, but he gave up his calling when his first wife died. To him, following a loving God meant life would go as planned: He'd marry, serve the church, raise a family, and live happily ever after. Then his wife got cancer. His circumstances, and ultimately her death, didn't fit with his image of God.

My professor viewed God as part indulgent grandfather (one who would give him what he wanted, as long as he behaved) and part mail-order clerk (pay for your goods through good deeds and sacrifice, then get what you paid for). He thought that by serving God faithfully, life would go as he planned.

When his wife died, his view of God changed. Now God was either powerless (God *couldn't* heal his wife) or God was cruel (God *wouldn't* heal his wife). He wanted no part of Him. Sadly, both views were far from the truth of what God says about Himself in His Word.

Ironically, the true God of the Bible could have carried my professor through his wife's sickness and death—if only he'd known Him as He really is (more on this in chapter 7). By losing sight of God's true character, my professor robbed himself of the consolation only God can bring.

. . . WE CONFUSE COMFORT WITH AN ABSENCE OF SUFFERING OR PAIN.

Forgetting God and misunderstanding who God is aren't the only barriers to experiencing God's comfort. Sometimes we think comfort means there will be no suffering or pain.

Several years ago, I asked my small group to pray for my comfort as I struggled with the heartache of raising a handicapped child.

"If you would just pray more, and pray in faith, your son would be healed," a well-meaning group member responded.

Though she meant well, her words cut deeply. I *did* pray for my bright-eyed, tow-headed, stroke-injured preschooler; I sometimes prayed without ceasing. I *did* have faith; I had no doubt, none whatsoever, that God could heal this child. Pray more? In faith? Her stinging words felt like accusation.

And accusation they were, though unintended. Implicit in her comment was the presupposition that good Christians don't suffer. And if good Christians don't suffer, a comforting God will end our suffering immediately, when we ask Him—"in faith."

The problem with this way of thinking is that it flies in the face of what Scripture clearly says:

- Jesus suffered, and we will share in His sufferings (Romans 8:17; 2 Corinthians 1:5; Hebrews 2:18).

- Suffering is a normal part of the Christian experience (1 Peter 4:12–13).

- Suffering can be part of God's will (1 Peter 4:19).

- God uses suffering to build Christlike character (Romans 5:3–5).

- God comforts us in our troubles (2 Corinthians 1:4).

- God may not remove the source of our suffering (2 Corinthians 12:7–10).

- God uses suffering to teach us to rely on Him (2 Corinthians 1:8–9).

- Suffering can display the work and glory of God (John 9:2–3).

Christians are never promised trouble-free lives. In fact, the opposite is true; we are told to expect troubles and hardship. Obedient, faithful, belief-filled Christians do, and will, suffer. Scripture promises, however, that God will comfort us in all our troubles. Biblically speaking, comfort is not the absence of suffering; it is the assurance of God's presence with us in our suffering.

When we seek refuge in the Fortress of God, we discover that God is always with us, surrounding us with the Curtain Wall of His Comfort. In all things, in all places, in all circumstances, God is there. Won't you take a moment to notice His presence? Ask Him to remind you that you aren't alone. Let His presence remove your fear and assure you that your suffering has purpose. Allow Him to comfort you. When you do, you experience His refuge.

-<+ PUTTING IT INTO PRACTICE +>-

Take some time to reflect on the list of "suffering" passages noted in the preceding paragraphs. Look up the passages listed and write each one out, word for word, in a journal or notebook. Read over what you have written. Which of the biblical descriptions of suffering surprise(s) you? In which do you find the most comfort? How many of these passages can you apply directly to your situation? In what way do they apply?

After reading through and meditating on these passages, how would you summarize what the Bible says about suffering and comfort?

Questions for Reflection

1. How do you define *comfort?* Where do you tend to seek comfort most?

2. When are you most tempted to forget God's presence? What steps can you take to better remember Him?

3. What comfort do you find in knowing that God is with you?

4. Read 2 Corinthians 1:3–11. How does this passage apply to your situation?

5. What good can come from suffering? What benefits of suffering have you experienced in your life?

5

QUENCHING OUR THIRST:
The Well of Renewal

A thousand voices clamor for our attention, and a thousand causes vie for our support. But until we have learned to be satisfied with fellowship with God, until He is our rock and our fortress, we will be restless with our place in the world.

ERWIN W. LUTZER
quoted in *Draper's Book of Quotations for the Christian World*

The Lord sets us longing and then completely satisfies us.

C. H. SPURGEON
The Treasury of David, vol. 1

To him who is thirsty I will give to drink without cost from the spring of the water of life.

JESUS
Revelation 21:6

Fully half of all Americans (Christians and non-Christians alike) seek "meaning and purpose in life," according to a recent survey reported by the Barna Research Group.[1] Despite unlimited access to books, articles, and on-line literature on spirituality, our souls thirst for something more.

But more what? The non-Christian, we know, ultimately longs for a restored relationship with God. But, as Christians already in relationship with Him, for what do we yearn? Consider the yearnings described in the Psalms:

> As the deer pants for streams of water, so my soul pants for you, O God. My soul thirsts for God, for the living God. (Psalm 42:1–2)

> O God, you are my God, earnestly I seek you; my soul thirsts for you, my body longs for you, in a dry and weary land where there is no water. (Psalm 63:1)

Like the Psalms' writers, we thirst for a deeper experience of God. We've tasted His presence, but tasks and trials keep us parched and longing. Where can we find relief? At the Well of Renewal. It's here in the courtyard (Bailey) behind God's Fortress walls. Come, drink from the Well. Lean against its cool, smooth fieldstone. Smell the crisp, sweet air rising from the waters below. Look into the depths of this Fortress wellspring. It is here that God Himself refreshes our souls.

THE PROCESS OF RENEWAL: 1. DRINK OF THE RIGHT WELL

Partaking of this refreshing and vital water is a four-part process. First, we must drink of the right well. Though God's refreshing spring is at our fingertips, we may be tempted to drink of other wells along the way. Scripture cautions, "My people have committed two sins: They have forsaken me, the spring of living water, and have dug their own cisterns, broken cisterns that cannot hold water" (Jeremiah 2:13).

God is our source of life; He alone provides renewal for His people. But, just like the people of Israel, we tend to seek renewal in other places. We foolishly drink from wells of our own making. What do these shallow wells look like?

Watch Out: Wells Poisoned with Performance

Some wells are poisoned with performance. At these wells we say: "If I could just do more . . . "

In the first years after I became a Christian, I thought the key to maintaining a healthy relationship with God was religious activity. So I dove into ministry projects galore: helping in the church nursery; hosting a small group; teaching Sunday school; making meals for those in need. While momentarily gratifying, these involvements didn't satisfy my soul.

Maybe I'm just not doing enough, I remember thinking. So I worked harder and added more to my "to do" list: I wrote vacation Bible school curriculum; I discipled other women; I served on ministry committees; I spent more time praying for needs. *If I just do more,* I thought, *God will surely show Himself to me and give me the spiritual boost that I need.*

The problem was that it simply didn't work. I did all the "spiritually correct" things, but my heart cried out for something deeper. On the outside, I seemed to have my spiritual act together. Inside, I longed for something more.

I had it all backwards. My busy schedule was ultimately an attempt to earn God's approval, when what I really needed was communion with Him. You see, doing things for God isn't the same thing as developing a relationship with Him. Renewal comes not when we do good things to build up our faith, but when we look to the one who gives us faith.

Watch Out: Wells Eroded with Escapism

Performance isn't the only false well that can lead us astray. Another kind of well is eroded with escapism. At these wells we say: "If I could just get away . . ."

A few years ago, heavy snows and a virulent flu season conspired with my usual midwinter blues to create major discouragement. I needed renewal and assumed that time alone with no kids, no appointments, and a break from commitments and daily demands would provide what I needed. I asked God to give me time away so I could spend time with Him. I asked for "space." He answered my prayer, but not how I expected.

Shortly after I prayed, Dan, then twelve, went sledding and promptly lost a battle between his sled, his foot, and a black walnut tree. A broken foot is tough for anyone, but it's especially hard when you have only one normal foot to begin with. Because of his cerebral palsy, Daniel is hemiplegic: one entire side of his body (foot included) doesn't work right. And which foot did he break? His *good* foot! That meant no school for him, and no "space" for me.

Ironically, I was studying refuge in God at the time, and realized that certain things replaced God as my refuge. In the course of my study, God seemed to speak quietly to my heart: "You've been longing for 'space,' child, but what you really need is Me." I prayed for escape, but God gave me something better: Himself.

I learned something precious that winter: God's ability to renew me isn't dependent on my having "space." He can restore me even in the whirlwind of busyness, children, injuries, and sickness, sometimes even more so. Instead of drinking from the well of escape, God reminded me to drink of Him.

Watch Out: Wells that Confuse God's Provision with God's Person

Escape is a second false well to which we fall prey. There is one more, and it is the most dangerous. The worst kind of wells confuse God's provision with God's person.

I recently read a story about a prekindergarten Sunday school class learning about Solomon's building of the temple from 1 Kings 7–8 and 2 Chronicles 2–7. While reading aloud to her students, the teacher paused to describe the temple's huge dimensions, lavish materials, and fine furnishings. She encouraged the children to close their eyes and picture this glorious building in their minds. While the children imagined the magnificent temple Solomon built for God, she explained that the "presence of the Lord filled the temple." The four- and five-year-olds' eyes popped open and grew wide with excitement; you could feel their anticipation of what was to come.

The seasoned teacher delighted in their enthusiastic response until she realized that their excitement wasn't over the fact that God had come to dwell in His temple; the children were excited by the thought of an enormous building filled with "presents" from God! You see, the children confused presence (God's person) with presents (God's gifts).[2]

We, sadly, are much like those children. We are more excited about what God gives to us than who He is. Scripture clearly tells us, however, that refuge is in God's person (Psalms 46:1; 62:8; 91:2). Renewal is found in Him.

Performance, escape, and confusing God's gifts for His person can provide momentary relief for our thirst, but they ultimately leave us unsatisfied. Drinking from any well, other than this Well of living water, won't lastingly quench our thirst. Jesus said, "Everyone who drinks this water will be thirsty again" (John 4:13).

What well provides lasting relief? Jesus continues, "But whoever drinks the water I give him will never thirst. Indeed, the water I give him will become in him a spring of water welling up to eternal life" (John 4:14). The living water Jesus provides is the only water that will fully satisfy our souls. How do we drink of Him?

THE PROCESS: 2. WE MUST PICK UP THE CUP

The tricky thing about cups is that you can't drink from them with other things in your hands. When seeking renewal, a good question to ask is, "What do I hold that can hinder renewal?" In other words, what can keep me from holding the cup? Here are just a few of the things I've had to leave at the Well: pride, doubt, distractions, and a "need" to understand. I first experienced this emptying of my hands after the twins' birth in 1984.

After we lost Daniel's twin brother, it was very hard for me to pray. I was emotionally weary and spiritually dried up. I felt like I needed to understand God's plan. I needed to know "why." Then a woman I barely knew, who'd lost a child of her own, gently admonished that, though I couldn't see how, God had accomplished His purpose for my son's life while he was yet in my womb. She reminded me that God was sovereign and that His ways were right and good. She helped me to see that I might never understand why He allowed my son to die, and encouraged me to shift my focus from "why" to "who." As a result, I began to focus on God's character and offered my need to understand as an offering of trust to Him. When I did, I was able to pray again, and God revived my soul.

Renewal came when I humbly relinquished my need to understand and picked up the cup of confidence: confidence in God's character and of my relationship with Him. A cup, however, won't sustain me in the long run. I need to drink deeply and continually from the Well.

THE PROCESS: 3. WE MUST DRINK DEEPLY

Consider what the prophet Jeremiah said: "When your words came, I ate them; they were my joy and my heart's delight" (Jeremiah 15:16). Jeremiah internalized God's Word; he drank deeply. Our problem is that we often view God's Word as an impersonal set of principles. We keep the Bible at arm's length and read it as we would a textbook or other nonfiction work. The psalmists had a different view:

The law of the LORD is perfect, reviving the soul. (Psalm 19:7)

I delight in your decrees; I will not neglect your word. (Psalm 119:16)

My soul is consumed with longing for your laws at all times. (Psalm 119:20)

How sweet are your words to my taste, sweeter than honey to my mouth! (Psalm 119:103)

God's Word was not a set of cold, objective facts to these writers; His Word was a wellspring of delight. We, too, can find satisfying joy in God's Word. How? Psalm 1:1–2 tells us, "Blessed is the man [whose] . . . delight is in the law of the LORD, and on his law he meditates day and night."

Satisfaction first comes when we know and reflect on God's Word. When the Bible moves from being head knowledge to heart knowledge it becomes our very sustenance, our source of life. Knowing Scripture enables us to drink continually of the living Word, Jesus.

There are many ways to internalize Scripture, even in our whirlwind lives:

- Listen to Scripture songs (even children's audiotapes will do).

- Use a "verse-a-day" calendar and put it where you'll see it (window sill above the kitchen sink, your desktop, a nightstand, etc.).

- Jot verses of Scripture on adhesive-backed notepaper, and stick them in visible places, such as the bathroom mirror, kitchen cupboard, dashboard, computer monitor, or office door.

- Keep spiral-bound index cards handy when you read Scripture. Jot down encouraging verses as you read them; then carry them with you. Review your verses while waiting in line at the grocery store or doctor's office.

- Memorize Scripture (try the NavPress Topical Memory System).

- Meditate (reflect in your mind) throughout the day on what you've read and heard.

Jesus reminds us, "You will know the truth, and the truth will set you free" (John 8:32). Knowing God's Word frees us to experience His renewal. It allows us to draw living water from Him.

If, however, we rely only on sporadic Bible study, our renewal will be temporary. How then do we experience the unending satisfaction of John 4:14?

THE PROCESS: 4. WE MUST DRINK CONTINUALLY

How? You may not like the answer: abiding prayer. This is not liturgical prayer on Sunday mornings or checklist prayers of distinct "quiet times." The prayer that provides ongoing access to our well-spring, Christ, is the unending prayer the apostle Paul mentions in his letters: "Pray continually" (1 Thessalonians 5:17); "Be . . . faithful in prayer" (Romans 12:12); "And pray . . . on all occasions with all kinds of prayers" (Ephesians 6:18). Jesus said, "Abide in Me" (John 15:4 NASB) and "Abide in My love" (John 15:9 NASB). To abide is simply to live with a continual awareness of God's presence.

In our fast-paced world, what does this abiding prayer look like?

- Thought prayers (thinking your prayers as you go about your daily tasks).
- Scripture prayers (repeating Scripture prayerfully to God).
- Prayer without words (action done to the glory of God).
- Listening prayer (quiet openness to God's voice).
- Breath thanks (spontaneous thanks offered to God "under your breath").
- Silent petition (lifting a need before God in the quiet of your heart).
- Momentary offerings (surrendering individual moments to God).
- Groaning prayer (longing for God).
- Prayers of tears (crying before God).
- "For Your glory" prayers (thinking "for Your glory" in the midst of the next difficulty, demand, or crisis).
- Singing prayers (singing hymns and other worship songs to God).

These are but a few of the ways we can drink deeply through abiding prayer. Notice that these are not done separately from the hubbub of living. We drink deeply of God in the ordinary moments of everyday life. Seventeenth century French monk Nicholas Herman of Lorraine (otherwise known as Brother Lawrence) described abiding prayer well:

> Since you cannot but know that God is with you in all you undertake, that He is at the very depth and centre of your soul, why should you not thus pause an instant from time to time in your outward business, and even in the act of prayer, to worship Him within your soul, to praise Him, to entreat His aid, to offer Him the service of your heart, and give Him thanks for all His loving-kindnesses and tendermercies?

> What offering is there more acceptable to God than thus throughout the day to quit the things of outward sense, and to withdraw to worship Him within the secret places of the soul?[3]

Continual renewal isn't just for spiritual giants of this world. It's for you and for me. The invitation stands: "The Spirit and the bride say, 'Come!' And let him who hears say, 'Come!' Whoever is thirsty, let him come; and whoever wishes, let him take the free gift of the water of life" (Revelation 22:17). Won't you come, then? Enter God's refuge and drink of His Well. Find renewal in Him!

-+- PUTTING IT INTO PRACTICE +>-

If we're not thirsty, we won't come to the Well. A.W. Tozer wrote, "The stiff wooden quality of our religious lives is the result of our lack of holy desire. Complacency is a deadly foe of all spiritual growth. . . . [God] waits to be wanted."[4]

How do we grow in wanting God? Take a moment now. Put this book down and be still. Close your eyes and quietly pray,

Father, show me the void in my heart. Show me the places where I've filled that void with things other than You. Create in me a longing for You that surpasses all other longings. Make me want to want You. In Jesus' name, amen.

That is a prayer God will say "yes" to. He wants us to want Him.

Questions for Reflection

1. Are you thirsty? For what do you thirst?

2. From which false wells have you drawn to satisfy your thirst?

3. What has kept you from drinking of the living Well of God? List those things on a sheet of paper. Now go over your list line by line and prayerfully give those things to God.

4. After reading this chapter, what does John 4:13–14 mean to you?

5. What one thing do you plan to apply from this chapter? How will you apply it?

Notes

1. Barna Research Online, "Most People Seek Control, Adventure, and Peace in Their Lives," 1 August 2000, at the web site www.barna.org; accessed on 26 November 2001.
2. Michael Hodgin, *1001 Humorous Illustrations for Public Speaking* (Grand Rapids: Zondervan, 1994), 373.
3. Brother Lawrence, *The Practice of the Presence of God with Spiritual Maxims* (Grand Rapids: Revell, 1967), 71–72.
4. A.W. Tozer, *The Pursuit of God* (Harrisburg, Pa.: Christian Publications, 1948), 17.

6

EXPECT THE UNEXPECTED:
The Storehouse of Provision

*We are often unable to tell people what they need . . .
because they want . . . something else.*

GEORGE MACDONALD
Phantastes and Lilith

-->->- -<-<-

Hope in God, who richly provides.

—1 TIMOTHY 6:17

And my God will meet all your needs according to his glorious
riches in Christ Jesus.

—PHILIPPIANS 4:19

During my college summers working with teenagers at a Christian camp, a key responsibility was to help lead out-of-camp wilderness trips. That included taking groups of fourteen-year-old girls safely down the rapids of the Youghiogheny River. Though the girls were eager to try white-water rafting, they simply weren't outdoorswomen. These were the same girls who'd planned to take hair dryers along on a three-day backpacking trip.

"Sorry, girls," I had to explain, "there are no electrical outlets in the middle of the woods!"

Before getting into our rafts, I would review some basic details:

"You must have your life vests on and secured at *all* times."

"If you get bucked out of the raft, rest on your back with your feet facing *downstream,* and allow the current and your life vest to carry you."

"An 'elephant' is a partially submerged obstruction that is visible above the water line; we need to steer clear of elephants."

"In the rapids, if the raft gets washed sideways up against a rock, *hug the rock.* Your instincts will tell you to jump away from the rock, but *lean into* the rock, or we will capsize."

Life jackets on, paddles in hand, we would hop into our raft and glide into the main flow of the river. I remember one trip in particular with my fourteen-year-olds. We had passed through the first few sets of rapids easily; everyone worked together and did as instructed. The girls splashed and giggled, and had the time of their lives. I laughed with them and enjoyed the splendor of God's creation.

Then we approached a more challenging class-three rapid: certainly passable, but dangerous nonetheless. A kayaker had recently drowned here when he mired upside down in the suction of the rapid's backwash. I'd warned my girls about backwashes and whirlpools, and I'd warned them about what to do if we were washed against a rock. We were ready.

After watching several other teen-filled rafts negotiate the whitewater without incident, my girls were confident and ready to go (although I had serious doubts about my hair-dryer-toting tenderfoots). Yelling over the roar of the river, I instructed them to keep paddling and to make a hard left at my command. Our goal was to get around an elephant in the middle of the river without mishap. We moved swiftly toward the looming boulder, dead on as we should. At just the right moment, I called for the hard left, the girls responded, and the nose of the raft went left (again, as it should). *We just might make it through,* I thought.

Then the girls saw the cascading water that marked the rest of our course. Frozen with fear, they all stopped paddling. With no one but me maneuvering our raft, we were at the mercy of the rainswollen river.

The powerful current swept us against the rock. We stuck fast. Jumping toward the boulder, I yelled, "Lean into the rock, girls!" And what did they do? Every last one moved away from the rock. There I was, a lone figure hugging this massive boulder while my five terrified campers scrambled to the raft's opposite side.

I could see the raft's inflated sides strain against the pulling vacuum. I screamed again, "HUG THE ROCK; YOU'VE GOT TO HUG THE ROCK!" Their instincts told them to do otherwise, so instead of listening to the voice of experience (in this case, my voice), they trusted their instincts. The result? Our raft flipped and all six of us were swept into the river's churning waters.

Trusting their instincts did not serve the girls well that day. Though we were later picked up safely several hundred feet downriver, we were bruised and shaken. The girls did learn something, however: Instinct is not always the best guide.

When we enter the Fortress of God, we discover the Storehouse of Provision. Though chock-full of all that we *need,* God's Storehouse may not provide what we *want* or *expect.* In fact, in my life, God's provision has been more like the instructions I gave to the girls on the raft trip that day: Instincts say one thing; He provides something else.

That wasn't usually the case in a medieval castle. A medieval storehouse held supplies for everyday life. If the castle cook needed wine for a banquet, grain for a meal, or salt pork for stew, he found it in the storehouse. Storehouses were predictable; what you came for is what you got (except when poor preservation resulted in rancid meat, moldy grain, or sour wine!). Generally speaking, there were few surprises.

A DIFFERENT KIND OF STOREHOUSE

God's provision is different. We won't always get what we ask for, but His something else is always for our good (no moldy grain or sour wine here). How can we be sure? God provides according to His wisdom, not ours. His provision flows from His good, loving character (more on that in chapter 7). His provision may not be what we want, or expect, or even what we request, but He is the one who knows our needs.

Second Peter 1:3 tells us, "His divine power has given us everything we need for life and godliness through our knowledge of him." Notice the all-encompassing nature of His provision: God provides *everything* we need for *life* and *godliness.* Wow! What a promise. He did the same for Elijah.

GOD'S PROVISION FOR ELIJAH

The Bible tells us little of Elijah's background or history, though we know that Elijah was God's prophet (His spokesman or mouthpiece) and that his walk with God was marked with many "victories." Among them: Elijah literally heard God's voice (1 Kings 17:2–4); he witnessed and participated in miracles (1 Kings 17:14–16; 18:19–40); when he prayed for a dead child, God brought the boy to life (1 Kings 17:20–23); and when he prayed for an end to a three-year drought, God sent rain (1 Kings 18:1, 42–45). When Elijah prayed, God responded!

You'd think Elijah's faith was unshakable.

Think again.

Just a few moments after Elijah's most visible ministry success (1 Kings 18:19–40), Queen Jezebel threatened him, and Elijah panicked and ran for his life. He fled to the desert in fear (see 1 Kings 19:1–4). There, thinking that death was the solution to his troubles, the weary prophet asked God to end his life.

God answered, but not in accordance with Elijah's prayer; instead He met his needs. Elijah was physically worn out. He'd hoofed over a hundred miles in a week's time with little, if any, rest (1 Kings 18:46 –19:4). When Elijah prayed to die, God heard him, but didn't do what he asked. Instead, He provided rest, food, and drink (1 Kings 19:5–7).

God didn't stop there; He also provided for the prophet's spiritual needs. God gave Elijah the gift of His tangible presence, but again, not in the way we expect. After so many displays of God's awesome might, we might assume God would reveal Himself in another demonstration of power. We read, however, that "the LORD was not in the wind. . . . The LORD was not in the earthquake. . . . The LORD was not in the fire" (1 Kings 19:11–12). God's presence was found in "a gentle whisper" (1 Kings 19:12–13). God came to Elijah in unexpected quietness, and in that quietness met his spiritual need.

God still wasn't done. He cared about Elijah's emotional health as well. The passage reveals Elijah's discouragement ("I am no better than my ancestors" [1 Kings 19:4]) and distorted sense of isolation ("I am the only one left" [v. 14]). But, again, God provided. God assured Elijah of the continuation of his work (vv. 15–16). He reminded Elijah of the truth of His faithfulness (v. 18) and designated Elisha to succeed Elijah as prophet (vv. 16–21). After years of isolation, Elijah would have an attendant by his side.

In a desert in Judah, when a depressed Elijah cried out to God, God heard him, but gave him something other than what he asked for. What is your need right now? Are you physically worn out like Elijah? Are you emotionally spent? Do the demands of your circumstances exceed your resources? When we seek refuge in our mighty God, we may not get what we want, but God will give what we need.

HOW TO EXPERIENCE GOD'S PROVISION

So how do we experience God's provision? We do what Elijah did.

Cry Out to God

First, we cry out to God. Elijah, despite his momentary panic, did the right thing. He went to God. We, too, can call upon God. We just need to go to Him and ask.

My poor husband! Instead of asking for help when I need it, I stubbornly try to do things myself (envision a two-year-old's cry, "Me do it!"), or I huff and puff until Don gets the hint that I want him to help me (envision big sighs, and pots and pans slamming to attract attention). I sometimes treat God the same way: hinting and sighing, but not asking directly. Silly me. Life would be so much simpler if I'd learn to ask for help.

James tells us that we don't have because we don't ask (James 4:2). How much more we would experience God's provision if we simply asked Him.

Wait

Second, after asking, we wait. What did Elijah do after he prayed? He made his request known and went to sleep! Granted, he was physically exhausted from the exertion of the previous week. He was also, in all likelihood, seriously depressed. But we don't see Elijah fretting about what God would do or how He would do it. And we don't see him attempting to "help" God answer his prayer.

Once, when he was five, Daniel asked me to pray for a special need. His lifelong best bud, a little girl named Liesel, had moved out of state, and Daniel missed her terribly. It had been several months since we'd heard from her or her family, so Daniel asked to pray that he would receive a letter from his friend that day. *Oh boy,* I thought. *What is this going to do to his faith when we pray and there's no letter?*

Despite my doubts, I reluctantly agreed. We prayed, and I began scrambling to make this work. Maybe I could fake Leisel's handwriting and sneak my forgery into the morning's mail. Maybe I could use one of Liesel's old letters and put it into a new envelope. I felt like Daniel's young faith was riding on this. God wasn't going to let him down if I had anything to do with it! Oh, my unbelieving heart.

In the middle of my planning, God intervened. *Am I big enough to do this small thing?* He seemed to speak to my heart. *Do you care about Daniel's faith more than I? Do you trust Me to supply his need?* Ouch.

I stopped scheming, repented, prayed again, and waited. Instead of trying to "help" God answer my son's innocent prayer, I rested. And, don't you know, God provided a letter from Liesel that very morning.

God has not always worked so clearly in my life. His provision is not always so easily seen. Some days there isn't a letter in the mailbox. Inevitably, when I trust Him and wait, He provides according to the real (not felt) need.

Jesus told us in Matthew 6:31–33, "Do not worry, saying, 'What shall we eat?' or 'What shall we drink?' or 'What shall we wear?' . . . Your heavenly Father knows that you need them. But seek first his kingdom and his righteousness, and all these things will be given to you." Paul added in Philippians 4:6–7, "Do not be anxious about anything, but in everything, by prayer and petition, with thanksgiving, present your requests to God. And the peace of God, which transcends all understanding, will guard your hearts and your minds in Christ Jesus." When we make our requests known, our souls can be still. Why? Because God knows our needs. When we seek Him, we can rest in the assurance that God knows and will provide.

Obey Him

Third, we obey what He tells us to do. In response to Elijah's plea, God sent an angel who twice told Elijah to eat and drink; twice the prophet complied (1 Kings 19:5–8). Later God told Elijah to stand on the mountain to watch Him pass by; Elijah obeyed, and was blessed with a glimpse of the Almighty. We, like Elijah, need to obey what God says, both in His Word and in those promptings He gives that are consistent with His Word.

My sister, Jean, experienced a dramatic illustration of what can happen when we obey God's promptings. As Jeanie scurried through a very busy day, a college friend whom she hadn't seen in quite some time kept coming to mind. She had the distinct impression that God was telling her to call her. She picked up the phone and dialed.

After several rings, a familiar, but groggy, voice answered. Apologetic about sleeping in the middle of the day, her friend explained that she'd inadvertently dozed off and now had a headache. They cut the conversation short.

Feeling foolish about calling, Jeanie wondered about the prompting she'd felt. Her urgency made no sense, until she received a phone call the next day.

"You know you saved my life when you called me yesterday," her college chum's now perky voice enthused with amazement. Apparently after hanging up, my sister's friend sleepily noticed that her German Shepherd wasn't acting right; the normally frisky canine seemed sluggish. It was then that she realized something was wrong. After a trip to the emergency room, she discovered that both she and her dog were in the early stages of carbon monoxide poisoning.

A malfunctioning heating system had spewed deadly carbon monoxide gas into the apartment. If the telephone hadn't awakened her, Jeanie's friend would, in all likelihood, have slumbered into eternity.

My sister's obedience saved her friend's life. Though our obedience may not have the same dramatic results, we can be sure that God will use our obedience to bring life to our souls, as He did with Elijah.

What do you need right now? What are you lacking? Don't be like my teenage rafters who, when facing a need, trusted their instincts and ended up wet. Rather, learn from Elijah. Cry out to God, wait in His presence, and then obey what He tells you. God may not give what you ask for. He will, however, provide what you need.

-+- PUTTING IT INTO PRACTICE -+-

In a journal or notebook, create a chart with four columns. Label the first column, "Date." Label the second column, "Wants." Label the third, "Needs," and the fourth, "How God Provided." List your prayer requests on the chart as they arise. Notice that the chart includes both wants and needs. God desires that we bring both to Him.

Once you've completed your list, set the list in your hands, then place your hands palms up on the table in front of you. Close your eyes, prayerfully offer the list to God, and rest silently before Him. Over the next few days and weeks, look for God's provision. Be especially alert to ways God provides that might not be what you want or expect. Note His provision in your journal. Your record will provide future encouragement as you recall what God has done.

Questions for Reflection

1. In what ways do you identify with Elijah?

2. At this moment, are your needs more physical, spiritual, or emotional?

3. God reoriented Elijah's perspective from what was false ("I am the only one left" [1 Kings 19:14]) to what was true (God had reserved seven thousand, 1 Kings 19:18 reports). What lies or distortions of the truth might you haven fallen prey to in your thinking? Ask God to correct those distortions with His truth.

4. How have you experienced God's provision? Describe a time when God's provision was different than what you asked for or expected.

5. Read Matthew 6:25–34. Which part of the passage speaks most to your heart?

PART TWO

The Middle Regions

—>—<—

In the storm the tree strikes deeper roots in the soil; in the hurricane the inhabitants of the house abide within, and rejoice in its shelter. So by suffering the Father would lead us to enter more deeply into the love of Christ.

—>—<—

ANDREW MURRAY
Abide in Christ

What drove you to seek refuge in God? When you crossed the Drawbridge and passed through the Gatehouse, what were you looking for? My guess is that you sought shelter from some storm in your life—a hurricane of pressure; a tornado of busyness, a blizzard of confusion, or an earthquake of life-shattering pain.

Storms drive us to seek deeper refuge. When we stepped inside the fortress walls we experienced the initial aspects of refuge in God—relief, comfort, renewal, and provision. But that experience was only a taste of what lies farther within. To experience deeper refuge, we must venture farther into the Fortress.

When we step through the doorway beyond the Bailey of Relief, we enter His Keep of Shelter; here our journey moves from the outer regions of what God does for us to the inner recesses of who God is. Come with me now as we seek shelter in the character of God.

7

A PLACE IN THE STORM:
The Keep of Shelter

The delight which the mariner feels, when . . . he steps again upon the solid shore, is the satisfaction of a Christian when . . . he rests the foot of his faith upon this truth—"I am the Lord, I change not."

C. H. SPURGEON
Morning and Evening

→►◄←

In the shelter of your presence you hide them.

—PSALM 31:20

You have been a refuge for the poor, a refuge for the needy in his distress, a shelter from the storm and a shade from the heat.

—ISAIAH 25:4

When I was a child, we spent our summers at my parents' lakeside cottage tucked away in the endless mountains of Pennsylvania's Susquehanna County. One of my favorite summertime ventures there was to grab a favorite book, row our old wooden boat out to the deepest part of the lake, curl up on the bow's boat cushions, and get lost in the fictional land of the day. The lake was usually calm, and with no motorized vehicles allowed, it was quiet; I could read undisturbed for hours on end.

On one such afternoon, I was absorbed in J. R. R. Tolkien's *The Hobbit* when a fast-moving thunderstorm blew in from the west. Because the lake is nestled beneath surrounding hills, it's nearly impossible to see storms approaching. I was so lost in my adventures with Bilbo Baggins that I didn't realize a storm had developed until lightning struck the shore. I suddenly found myself in the middle of the lake with the storm closing in (definitely not a good place to be).

All I could think of was that I needed shelter. I jumped up from my reading, rammed the oars into the oarlocks, and started rowing hard. The oarlocks groaned and waves lapped the bow as my ten-year-old arms pulled and strained to make headway against the wind. Just when I reached the dock, I heard the unmistakable roar of pouring rain. I turned and looked; sure enough, I saw a wall of water pelting the lake's surface as the storm advanced toward me across the lake. In just a few seconds, I'd be drenched, and who knows where the next lightning strike would be.

I threw the boat's tattered rope around the dock post,

grabbed my book, scrambled up the fieldstone steps, and sprinted to the cottage. Just as the screen door slammed behind me, the storm raged its full fury against the cabin walls.

DRIVEN TO SHELTER

Storms have a way of driving us to shelter, though it isn't just physical storms that cause us to flee. Circumstantial storms can also cause us to seek a place to hide. In Psalm 31:20, the psalmist sought shelter from "the intrigues of men" and "accusing tongues." In other passages, the writers sought shelter from enemies, heat, storms, and "the breath of the ruthless" (Isaiah 25:4). Accusation, betrayal, persecution, tragedy—these can drive us to shelter, too.

What is shelter? When we talk about shelter in the physical sense (as in seeking shelter from hail or lightning or driving rain), we mean protection from the elements. When I ran into the cottage, it kept me safe and dry, untouched by the storm outside. This kind of shelter provides physical protection that, hopefully, keeps us safe from injury or harm. Though physical protection may be possible, this is *not* the typical shelter we find in the Fortress of God.

The shelter we experience in God's Mighty Fortress is a shelter for the heart. Troubling circumstances can cause internal storms (both spiritual and emotional) that rage deep within our souls— storms of fear, doubt, or confusion; of worry, heartache, or loss. These storms, if allowed to batter our hearts unchecked, could ultimately damage our faith. We need an internal shelter to which we can flee when spiritual or emotional storms threaten to overtake us. Psalm 91:1 says, "He who dwells in the shelter of the Most High will rest in the shadow of the Almighty." We find a shelter for our souls in our God Most High.

In our journey so far, we've discovered something of what God does for us when we seek refuge in Him. Many Christians mistakenly stop their journey here. Sadly, these outer-region dwellers miss the greatest treasure of refuge: discovering *who God is*. To discover this treasure, we must risk moving beyond the castle's outer regions into the sheltering Keep. We must allow the storms to drive us on. That is the gift of storms; storms drive us from the Fortress's comfortable outer regions into the Sheltering Keep of the Person of God.

ABOUT THE KEEP

The castle keep was a large, square building, two to four stories tall, supported by thick, impregnable walls, and found deep within the fortress. When the castle came under attack or siege, castle dwellers fled into the keep for defense, safety, and hiding. The keep, almost always made of mighty stone, was like a mini fortress within a fortress, a strong refuge.

The keep, however, was only as reliable as its foundation. If built on a dirt or sand foundation, the sturdy keep was still vulnerable to flooding or enemies tunneling underneath. If the foundation was wood, enemies could catapult tar onto the wood, shoot burning arrows, and set it aflame. If, on the other hand, the keep's foundation was cut out of rock or carved of stone, the keep provided secure and reliable shelter.

The Bible repeatedly refers to God as a "rock" (Deuteronomy 32:4; Psalm 18:2; 62:7; 94:22; Isaiah 17:10; 44:8). Our shelter is cleft in Him. His name "is a strong tower; [where] the righteous run . . . and are safe" (Proverbs 18:10). We find protection for our faith and shelter from internal storms in the rock-solid nature of God. While it is impossible to fully address His nature in this book, five foundational attributes of God provide key shelter from emotional and spiritual onslaughts. What is an attribute of God? It is "whatever God has in any way revealed as being true of Himself."[1]

GOD'S FOUNDATIONAL ATTRIBUTE 1: LOVE

First, God is Love; He wants to provide shelter. When my children were small, middle-of-the-night thunderstorms brought scenes reminiscent of the Von Trapp children in *The Sound of Music*. Each lightning strike sent one more little one scurrying to our room. Did we relish the idea of three squirming kids sharing our bed and disturbing our much-needed sleep? No, but we loved them. We *wanted* to be their shelter in the storm. Our love prompted us to care for our children, though our love was imperfect.

Imagine the kind of shelter a perfect Father would provide, one whose love is unfailing and abounding (Psalm 48:9; 86:15), one who "lavishes" His love on His sons and daughters (1 John 3:1), and one whose love "endures forever" (Psalm 136). Imagine a Father who takes great delight in His children and quiets them with His love (Zephaniah 3:17). Do you think that Father would want to provide shelter for His loved ones? Would He be pleased when His children sought shelter with Him? This is the kind of Father we have in God, and that's how He loves us. We can be confident that God wants to provide refuge for us because He is love (1 John 4:8).

GOD'S FOUNDATIONAL ATTRIBUTE 2: STRENGTH

Second, God is strong; He is able to provide shelter. Notice what Scripture says about God's ability: "Lord, you have made the heavens and the earth by your great power and outstretched arm. Nothing is *too hard for you*" (Jeremiah 32:17, italics added). Job said, "I know that you *can do all things;* no plan of yours can be thwarted" (Job 42:2, italics added). God Himself has said, "Is anything too hard for the LORD?" (Genesis 18:14). God doesn't only want to provide shelter; He is *able* to do so.

Do you remember the old playground argument between two boasting children?

"My daddy is stronger than your daddy!"

"No, my daddy is stronger than yours!"

"Oh yeah? Well, my daddy is the strongest daddy in the whole wide world!"

Each child felt secure because he was confident in his daddy's strength and ability. When bullies threatened, he found emotional shelter in what his daddy could do.

God is the "Lord Almighty" (Psalm 24:10; 89:8; Jeremiah 50:34). He has power to save (Zephaniah 3:17). He is a strong fortress to which we can flee (Psalm 31:2). Our "Daddy" (Romans 8:15) is the strongest Daddy in all of creation! Our hearts can find shelter in what He can do.

GOD'S FOUNDATIONAL ATTRIBUTE 3: FAITHFULNESS

Third, God is faithful; He will *provide shelter.* One my favorite illustrations of faithfulness comes from the delightful Dr. Seuss fable
Horton Hatches the Egg. Horton, a gentle, kindhearted elephant, is
talked into sitting on a bird's nest because the mother bird feels she
needs a rest from her egg-sitting duties. Mayzie, "the lazy bird,"
assures Horton that she won't be gone long, so Horton promises to
"sit softly" on her egg until her return. Mayzie, however, doesn't
return quickly. She travels the world while poor Horton waits on the
top of a tree for months on end.

Horton knows that the life of the hatchling beneath him is
dependent upon his staying on the nest, so through foul weather,
storms, and considerable ridicule, Horton keeps his promise. Horton defends his decision to stay on the nest by saying, "I meant what
I said and I said what I meant. . . . An elephant's faithful one hundred per cent!"[2]

We live in a world full of Mayzies. People break promises and let
us down. The good news is that God will never betray us! God keeps
His promises and does what He says. Hebrews 6:18 assures us that
it is impossible for God to lie. In other words, God is faithful. Our
God is the God of 100-percent faithfulness. He keeps His word.
We can trust Him to provide shelter because He has said He will.

GOD'S FOUNDATIONAL ATTRIBUTE 4: GOODNESS

Fourth, God is good; His shelter is good. The Psalms are filled with
statements recounting God's goodness (for example, Psalms 31:19;
119:68; 145:7), but what do we mean when we say God is good?

English dictionaries define "good" as beneficial, virtuous, just,
commendable, loyal, and having praiseworthy character (among
other things). In Scripture, God's "goodness" suggests that God is
morally right, correct, and gracious in all His ways.[3] A. W. Tozer
defines God's goodness this way: "God is kindhearted, gracious,
good-natured, and benevolent in intention. . . . God has . . . a heart
infinitely kind and . . . there is no boundary to it."[4]

All too often I hear Christians describe God as a score-keeping cosmic killjoy who delights in faultfinding. If that were the case, I certainly wouldn't have any interest in seeking shelter in Him. Who would want shelter in that kind of God? But that is not the God of the Bible. The God of the Bible is gracious and kind. The God of the Bible is morally upright and correct in all His ways. The God of the Bible is good.

Our problem is that our definition of good differs from His. When we say "God is good," we sometimes mean that God is indulgent—He gives us what we want—or that God is a handyman—He will fix our problems. *If God is good,* we reason, *He will protect us from hardship.* God's goodness, however, serves a higher purpose than providing things that please or satisfy. His ultimate good involves bringing sinners to salvation and molding believers into the image of His Son. God's primary concern for me is not that I be comfortable; it is that I become Christlike.

When we see God's goodness in light of His ultimate purposes, we begin to realize that to say "God is good" doesn't mean He will remove our suffering or end our pain. It means, rather, that He will use the storm for His good intent. The shelter His goodness provides is the knowledge that, though storms rage and we may not understand God's ways, we can be confident that He is upright in all His dealings with us.

GOD'S FOUNDATIONAL ATTRIBUTE 5: SOVEREIGNTY

Fifth, God is sovereign; we find shelter in His control. Best-selling author Philip Yancey provides a window into God's sovereignty by describing a chess match he played with a superior chess player:

> When we played a few matches, I learned what it is like to play against a master. . . . Although I had complete freedom to make any move I wished, I soon reached the conclusion that none of my strategies mattered very much. His superior skill guaranteed that my purpose inevitably ended up serving his own.

. . . When a Grand Master plays a chess amateur, victory is assured no matter how the board may look at any given moment. In a miracle of grace, even our personal failures can become tools in God's hands.[5]

When the Bible says that God is sovereign, it means that God reigns no matter what moves we make or what happens to us on the chessboards of our lives. God is in control, orchestrating all the events and details of our lives to accomplish His good purpose. When we understand that God is sovereign over *everything* that happens to us, good and bad, our hearts can withstand even the worst tempest or trial.

One caveat: Finding shelter in God's character doesn't mean the sun will shine or the rains will end. When I found shelter in the cottage that summer day, the storm had only begun. Old Testament figure David sought shelter *in times of trouble* (Psalm 59:16). God's prophet Isaiah described God's shelter *in the storm* (Isaiah 25:4). Though there will be a day when all storms shall cease (Revelation 21:3–4), and though we long for that day, in this life the storms go on.

WHAT KEEPS US FROM SHELTER?

If all of the above is true—if God wants to, is able, and is willing to provide refuge, and if He truly is good and always in control— why do we struggle to find shelter in Him? Let me suggest three things:

1. *We don't really know God.* Unlike my sociology professor (chapter 4), this isn't a matter of holding the wrong view of God; it is not knowing who He is to begin with. Scottish preacher, scholar, and author George MacDonald once said, "To say, 'Thou art God,' without knowing what the 'thou' means—of what use is it? God is a name only except we know God."[6] When we haven't taken the time to learn what God says about Himself in His Word, God is, indeed, a

name only. For Him to be our refuge, He must be more than a name to us.

2. *We rely on selective knowledge.* In other words, we know God, but we focus on a single aspect of God's character to the exclusion of others. For example, if I believe God is sovereign, but not that He is good, I may be tempted to think, *Yes, He's in control, but He's out to harm me.* Or if I believe that God is loving, but not strong, I might think, *God cares, but He can't really do anything.* When we approach God's character as a pick-and-choose buffet, we lose the complete picture. A true picture of God includes all that He has said He is. Selective beliefs that limit God rob us of the shelter that could be ours.

3. *We don't believe God.* Our experience of refuge depends on both the truth of who God is *and* how we view that truth. The reliability of God's character is without question, but do I believe He is who He claims to be? Am I certain God is good? Do I have confidence in His strength? Do I trust He is sovereign? If I don't believe what God says about Himself, I have no foundation upon which to build shelter in Him.

A CALM SHELTER

The Keep of Shelter, founded on the biblical character of God, is truly a place of shelter for our hearts. Though the storms rage outside, our hearts can hide in the loving faithfulness of our good and sovereign God. Take some time now to evaluate. On what do you build your confidence? What foundation supports your sense of well-being? On what have you grounded your faith?

Twentieth-century British preacher Martyn Lloyd-Jones once stated, "If our quietness of heart depends . . . upon any individual human being, upon our family, our home, our profession, our money, our health and strength, we are doomed to disappointment."[7] These are unreliable shelters. Only a keep built on the truth of God's character will provide a reliable place to flee. When we run to the Mighty Fortress of our unchanging God, His character becomes our shelter in the storm. When the winds howl and the rains come, where will you hide?

⤙ PUTTING IT INTO PRACTICE ⤚

Number a sheet of notebook paper from one to thirty-one. Next to each number, list an attribute, name, or characteristic of God described in the Bible. Use your list for one month to reflect on a different attribute of God each day. (Try these passages to give you a start: Psalm 8; Psalm 27; Psalm 46; Isaiah 6:1–7; Isaiah 9:6; Lamentations 3:22–25; Nehemiah 9:31; Matthew 11:29; John 1:14).

If thirty-one days is too much for you right now, try seven. List the days of the week on the left side of your paper. Then, for each day, list an attribute of God that begins with the same letter as that day of the week (e.g.: Monday— Majestic, Tuesday—True, Wednesday—Wise, Thursday— Trustworthy, etc.). Reflect on these attributes daily for the next seven days, and then repeat the process.

Questions for Reflection

1. Would you say that your faith is grounded more on feelings (what you feel about God) or facts (what the Bible says about God)?

2. How is God's character related to experiencing refuge in Him?

3. With which of God's attributes are you most familiar? Which would you like to study further?

4. Of the three reasons listed for not experiencing shelter, which best explains your own difficulty to experience shelter in God?

5. Which of God's attributes is most meaningful to you? Why?

Notes

1. A. W. Tozer, *The Knowledge of the Holy* (New York: Harper & Row, 1975), 20.
2. Dr. Suess, *Horton Hatches the Egg* (New York: Random House, 1968), 18.
3. R. Laird Harris, Gleason L. Archer Jr., and Bruce K. Waltke, eds., *Theological Wordbook of the Old Testament,* 2 vols. (Chicago: Moody, 1980), 1:345–46.
4. A. W. Tozer, *The Attributes of God* (Camp Hill, Pa.: Christian Publications, 1997), 42–43.
5. Philip Yancey, "Chess Master," *Christianity Today,* 22 May 2000, 112.
6. George MacDonald, *George MacDonald: 365 Readings,* ed. C. S. Lewis (New York: Collier, 1947), 14.
7. Martyn Lloyd-Jones, *Be Still My Soul* (Ann Arbor, Mich.: Servant, 1995), 83.

8

ONE STEP AT A TIME:
The Staircase of Growth

[A Christian] may be and often is highest when he feels lowest and most sinless when he is conscious of sin.

A. W. TOZER
That Incredible Christian

+>-<+

The path of the righteous is like the first gleam of dawn, shining ever brighter till the full light of day.

—PROVERBS 4:18

For sin shall not be your master, because you are not under law, but under grace.

—ROMANS 6:14

Do you remember "warm fuzzies"? For those who grew up with the Jesus Movement of the late '60s and early '70s, "warm fuzzies" described the smiley-faced, warm-feeling words we said to each other. We wanted to make others feel good by saying nice things. Constructive criticism, negative feedback, honest challenges, confronting truth, even in love—these were "cold pricklies," to be avoided at all cost. They were "bad vibes" to the "good vibrations" generation.

So far, we've remained in the "warm fuzzy" regions of our Fortress; we've enjoyed relief, comfort, renewal, provision, and shelter. These aspects of refuge feel good; they sweetly soothe our souls. Now it's time to move inward. For us to truly experience God's deepest refuge, we must be willing to take the challenging, sometimes uncomfortable climb up the Staircase of Growth. This ascent may not always be pleasant—it will, at times, bring tears—but it is where we must go to continue our journey. We won't avoid "cold pricklies" here.

In the previous chapter, we found a reliable place of retreat; shelter in the Keep of God's attributes. When we dwell in the Keep for more than just a cursory moment, something unexpected happens: As we delight in who God is, we begin to sense something raw gnawing at our hearts. God is revealing the sin that resides in us still. He's leading us toward the Staircase of Growth.

When we first stepped into the Keep, we didn't notice the illuminated doorway exiting the Keep's far corner. With each new attribute of God we discovered, we drew nearer to the Door. There is something different about this doorway; its light is almost blinding. It frightens us, but we press on, drawn by God's goodness and love. We come to the exit, and, while shielding our eyes, we squint to read the sign posted above the Door: *holiness.*

EMBRACING *ALL* GOD IS

By embracing the *true* God of the Keep, we embrace *all* of who He is. That includes those aspects of God that terrify us. When the biblical prophet Isaiah saw God in a vision, he responded, "Woe to me! . . . I am ruined! For I am a man of unclean lips, and I live among a people of unclean lips, and my eyes have seen the King, the LORD Almighty" (Isaiah 6:5). When the apostle John, the disciple "whom Jesus loved" (John 21:7, 20), saw his Lord in a vision, he fell at Jesus' feet "as though dead" (Revelation 1:17). God's holiness results in our falling on our faces before Him. Why?

The brilliance of God's holiness reveals dark vestiges of sin hiding in our souls. When we see the truth of His character, and the truth of who we are before Him, we can't help but see more of our sin and be overcome with the bittersweet grief that leads to repentance. Fourteenth-century mystic Julian of Norwich captured this process well: "Our Lord God in his mercy shows us our sin and our feebleness by his own sweet gracious light; for our sin is so vile and so horrible that out of his courtesy he will not show it to us save in the light of grace and mercy."[1]

God's holiness reveals our sin, but always in the context of His grace and mercy. This is a surprising aspect of refuge for those who risk moving beyond the exterior regions of our Fortress. We may not expect reminders of our ugly sinfulness from a loving God, but His holiness always lets us see clearly our sinful selves and the need for a Savior.

Though this aspect of refuge may wound you, press on. Allow God to draw you through the Door of His holiness into the Staircase of Growth. It is well worth the pain.

ASCENDING THE STAIRCASE

When we pass through the Door of God's holiness, we see it illuminates the Staircase of Growth. This is the spiral staircase found in the corner tower attached to the Keep. It leads to the Fortress's highest rooms and is our only path to deeper refuge. When we ascend the Staircase, we grow.

Spiritual growth, however, doesn't begin here. We started growing the minute we crossed the Drawbridge and entered the Fortress. When God's Walls surrounded us with comfort, we grew in awareness of Him. When we surrendered our burdens, we grew in broken dependence on Christ. When we drank of the Well, we learned to abide in Christ in everyday life. We are already growing! And when we hid in the Keep we grew in knowledge of God.

Just stepping into the Keep, however, didn't reveal the one attribute of God that most affects our spiritual growth. We needed to walk through the Keep and pass through the Door of God's holiness. As puritan John Howe once stated, holiness is the "attribute of attributes."

Scripture emphasizes God's holiness in a way it does no other. It is the only attribute of God repeated consecutively three times in Scripture: "Holy, holy, holy is the LORD Almighty"(Isaiah 6:3). It is the only attribute by which God swears His truthfulness: "Once for all, I have sworn by my holiness—and I will not lie to David" (Psalm 89:35). Holiness further defines God's other attributes: God's love is holy love; God's strength is holy strength; God's power is holy power. It is the attribute that most fully describes who God is. What do we mean when we say God is holy?

In his theological treatise *The Existence and Attributes of God,* Stephen Charnock described holiness this way: "The holiness of God . . . is a perfect and unpolluted freedom from all evil. As we call gold pure that is not embased by any dross, and that garment clean that is free from any spot, so the nature of God is estranged from all shadow of evil, all imaginable contagion."[2] Arthur Pink defined holiness similarly, "In Scripture [God] is frequently styled 'The Holy One': He is so because the sum of all moral excellency is found in Him. He is absolute Purity, unsullied even by the shadow of sin."[3]

Scripture tells us that "God is light; in him there is no darkness at all" (1 John 1:5). Holiness, though impossible for our finite minds to fully explain or comprehend, has something to do with the complete absence of evil in the character of God. He is morally perfect, without sin, and because He is so, He cannot ignore, overlook, excuse, or approve of evil. God, because He is holy, necessarily hates sin, even sin in the life of the refuge-seeking believer.

Why is this attribute so important to our growth? God's holiness reveals the magnitude and gravity of our sin, not just at salvation, but as Christians continually battling a sin nature (Romans 7). When His holiness reveals the seriousness of our sin's offense and its pervasiveness in our lives (both in attitude and action), we realize how desperately we need God to forgive, deliver, and change us. He responds with grace, and His grace becomes dearer to us. The more precious God's grace becomes, the more motivated we are to yield to and pursue Him. The more we pursue God, the more we see of His holiness, and the cycle continues. It's an ongoing spiral of growth that draws us ever nearer to God. The process is depicted in "The Spiral Staircase of Growth":

Figure 1: The Spiral Staircase of Growth

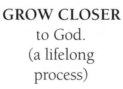

SEE GOD ACCURATELY
Glimpse God's character and understand He is holy.

YIELD & PURSUE
Yield to His Spirit's work in us, desire to please God, and hunger to know Him.

GROW CLOSER
to God.
(a lifelong process)

SEE SELF ACCURATELY
Understand we are sinful and in need of forgiveness.

REPENT
Experience God's grace and accept His forgiveness.

The Staircase of Growth is really a fourfold process: (1) seeing God accurately, (2) understanding who we are before Him, (3) responding appropriately, and (4) developing a hunger for God. The responding appropriately part is key to our growth.

RESPONDING APPROPRIATELY

When we seek refuge in God, glimpse His holiness, and begin to become aware of our sin, we have three choices: ignore our sin (deny that it exists or that it is sin), minimize our sin (not take it seriously), or see it for what it is and repent of it. When we repent, we experience God's forgiveness and yield more to His Spirit. As we yield and pursue God, His grace will draw us nearer than before.

In a small group I was involved in several years ago, one woman I'll call Sue regularly tried to monopolize our discussions with barbed complaints about her husband. Her angry, judgmental comments turned into husband-bashing gripe fests, which stifled and damaged our group dynamic. As the group leader, I needed to look out for the needs of the group, so I called and arranged to meet with Sue one-on-one.

As gently as possible, I expressed my love for Sue and my desire for her to remain in the group. I affirmed her struggle with a difficult marriage. I recommended counseling, and offered to make a few phone calls for her. But I also lovingly confronted her about the sin of her critical spirit and its impact on the other women.

Her response? First, she said, "But I'm not criticizing. I'm just being honest about my frustration." She defensively denied that her husband-bashing was sin.

Next, she said, "What's the big deal anyway? We all complain about our husbands now and then. God doesn't mind if I blow off some steam." She minimized both the offense of her sin before God, and its destructive impact on others.

Finally, after working together through the issues of "What is sin, really?" and "How does God view sin?" she began to see her harmful words for what they were. What helped her turn the corner? She began to "look upon all sin as that which crucified the Saviour and [she saw] it to be exceedingly sinful."[4]

Graciously, she repented and asked God to change her. She also asked for forgiveness not only from God, but from her husband and our small group. What followed was incredible. Recognizing her sin and allowing it to drive her to God turned her relationship with God around. God gave her a desire for Himself unlike any she'd known. Her relationship with Him grew, and as it did, her heart softened toward her husband. Though her marriage problems weren't solved, as God worked in the heart of this woman, her response to her situation improved.

How different the outcome would have been had she remained in denial or minimization!

WHEN WE IGNORE OR MINIMIZE SIN

Let's face it: If we ignore or minimize sin, our journey stops here. Sin keeps us from moving deeper into our fortress. The apostle John wrote, "If we claim to be without sin, we deceive ourselves and the truth is not in us. . . . If we claim we have not sinned, we make [God] out to be a liar and his word has no place in our lives" (1 John 1:8, 10). If we live as if God is a liar and His Word has no place in our lives, we cannot experience His refuge. Oh, how sinful we really are! How desperately we need forgiveness, even in times of refuge!

But, there is hope. Sandwiched between these two passages is grace-filled 1 John 1:9, "If we confess our sins, he is faithful and just and will forgive us our sins and purify us from all unrighteousness." We have simply to agree with God that we've sinned and ask God's forgiveness. He will forgive us and cleanse us from unrighteousness. God's cleansing makes us desire Him more, and we ascend one more step up the stairs.

THREE FALSE EXPECTATIONS THAT TRIP US

Climbing the Staircase is difficult enough, but be careful not to make it harder than it needs to be. Beware of expectations that can cause you to stumble.

1. Growth is fast.

If we expect to skip up the stairs, we're in for a rude awakening. Growth is hard work and takes endurance. We must remember that growth is a process, not an event. It is an ongoing battle, the progress of which is best measured by years (not weeks or months).

A good question to ask is, "How am I doing compared to a year ago? Two years ago? Five years? Ten years?" Don't trip over expecting microwave growth from a slow-cooker process.

2. Growth means that I won't struggle with sin.

The apostle Paul admitted, "I do not understand what I do. For what I want to do I do not do, but what I hate I do" (Romans 7:15). Remember, this is Paul speaking: the Hebrew-of-Hebrews Paul; the dramatic-conversion-on-the-road-to-Damascus Paul; the persecuted-preacher Paul whom God used to establish His church worldwide. Yes, even Paul wrestled with sin. And, like Paul, we will battle sin for the rest of our natural lives.

But God doesn't abandon us in the battle. He gives us His Spirit (Galatians 5:16–25; Romans 8:1–17). Without the Spirit's work in us, we would be unable to obey God, please Him, or resist sin's influence. God, again, out of His great mercy and love for us, gives us His Spirit. When we live by the Spirit's influence, we don't have to be controlled by our sinful nature.

Imagine God's holiness and grace drawing you up the stairs. At the start of the climb you notice a window on the sunny south side of the tower. As you pass the window, God's light reveals some specific sin or sinful attitude. You ask God's forgiveness, pray for His help, yield to His Spirit's influence, and move on. You continue your spiraling climb to the second and third stories, and with each new floor you discover another window, and more sin, on the same sunny south side. With each look through the window you discover that the moat, the trees, the mountains—everything outside is growing smaller; you're moving farther and farther away.

Much like our view from the tower windows, sin doesn't disappear, but its influence diminishes as we grow closer to God and walk in step with His Spirit (Galatians 5:25). In other words, as we grow, although we revisit particular sin issues, we confront them from a position of added growth and higher maturity.

3. My growth will be like everyone else's.

Because we are all different, our rate of growth will be different. We have different temperaments, personalities, and even capacities for stress and suffering. Your growth won't be like everyone else's.

One summer I climbed Paris' Notre Dame Cathedral. That's when I first realized spiral staircases could be challenging: Its tight, spiral staircase made me dizzy and disoriented. With nearly four hundred steps, it punished my lungs and thighs. The dark, windowless ascent blinded me to any progress I made. And the never-ending pressure of the crowd behind made it impossible to rest.

My experience in the French fortress town of Fougères was much different. Unlike Notre Dame, in Fougères tourists were permitted to climb the towers at will (no timed excursions). As an off-the-beaten-path attraction, there were few tourists to contend with; on the day we visited, we were the only ones there.

What fun we had! This spiraling staircase climb lacked the pressure found in the Notre Dame Cathedral. The staircase had its difficulties, of course. But when our legs hurt, we stretched them. When we grew tired, we paused for rest. With plentiful windows, the stairwells seemed light and airy, easily revealing how high we climbed. What freedom it was to explore at a rate suited to us!

Spiritual growth can be viewed like climbing either stairway: "Notre Dame growth" characterized by competitive standards (climb at the rate of the crowd) and end results (did you make it to the top); or "Fougères growth" characterized by individual standards (climb at the pace God designs for you) and which values the process (look how far He's brought you). Notre Dame growth emphasizes solutions and accomplishment; Fougères growth pursues perseverance and faithfulness.

What kind of growth do you expect? Refuge won't be found in Notre Dame growth. Why? We differ from each other. When wrestling with spiritual growth, we experience refuge when we realize that our walks with God will vary from time to time and from person to person.

I will have summer seasons of incredible growth, but I will also have winters of rest and preparation. You may be in the autumn's harvest, while I may be in the plantings of spring. Though every believer should display evidence of continual growth, we grow according to God's timing, not ours.

ACCEPTING GOD'S PACE FOR GROWTH

God is the one who produces growth in a heart. We can't make it happen for ourselves. Scripture tells us that God is faithful to accomplish what He began in each of us. He will bring His work to completion (Philippians 1:6; 1 Thessalonians 5:24). We don't have to climb like the next guy, nor do we have to force him up the stairs. We can rest while we climb, knowing that God works in us (and others) according to His plan and time.

We've discovered another surprising aspect of refuge, haven't we? Not only did we learn that refuge can bring an uncomfortable—but greatly beneficial—spiral of repentance and growth; we also discovered that growth happens according to the pace God sets for us. Hebrews 12:1 sums it up best: "Therefore, since we are surrounded by such a great cloud of witnesses, let us throw off everything that hinders and the sin that so easily entangles, and let us run with perseverance the race marked out for us."

We each have a race marked out before us, and that race includes the Staircase of Growth. Go ahead, throw off sin that entangles, ascend the Tower with perseverance, but do so according to the pace and parameters God establishes for you. You'll find deeper refuge as you climb.

⤙ PUTTING IT INTO PRACTICE ⤚

In your journal, list one sin issue that seems to be a chronic struggle for you. While remembering that Jesus perfects our faith, take an honest look at yourself. Where are you in the growth continuum regarding this sin? How do you view it? Do you take it seriously? Have you made any progress?

Take a moment now to reflect on God's holiness. How does He view that sin? Recognize the affront it is to God, ask His forgiveness, delight in His grace, ask the Spirit to work in you, yield, and move on up the stairs. Remember growth is a slow, steady process requiring ruthless perseverance concerning our sin.

Don't minimize or deny, but also don't be discouraged if your growth takes time. As an old Chinese proverb says, "Be not afraid of growing slowly; be afraid only of standing still."

Questions for Reflection

1. What does it mean that God is holy?

2. How does knowing that God is holy change your view of sin?

3. Do you most often tend to deny, minimize, or respond appropriately to your sin?

4. Have you ever experienced the pressure of competitive growth? When?

5. How might spiritual growth impact your experience of refuge?

Notes

1. Julian of Norwich, *Revelation of Love,* ed. and trans. John Skinner (New York: Doubleday, 1996), 169.
2. Stephen Charnock, *The Existence and Attributes of God* (Grand Rapids: Baker, 1981), 1:114–15.
3. Arthur W. Pink, *The Attributes of God* (Grand Rapids: Baker,1975), 41.
4. Charles Haddon Spurgeon, *Morning and Evening: Daily Readings* (Grand Rapids: Zondervan, 1976), 142 (March 11).

9

WONDER IN WEAKNESS:
The Tower of Strength

Are you mourning over your own weakness? Take courage. . . . Your emptiness is but the preparation for your being filled, and your casting down is but the making ready for your lifting up.

C. H. SPURGEON
Morning and Evening

→►◄←

That is why, for Christ's sake, I delight in weaknesses, in insults, in hardships, in persecutions, in difficulties. For when I am weak, then I am strong.

—2 CORINTHIANS 12:10

Weakness was turned to strength.

—HEBREWS 11:34

When we began our ascent up the Staircase of Growth, little did we realize how much strength we would need for our journey. Nor did we realize how deceptive the climb would be. Dutch graphic artist M. C. Escher, known for his artistic illusions, draws a fortress stairway entitled "Ascending and Descending," which illustrates our growth well. If you follow the steps in this impossible picture, you discover that though the steps appear to go up and down, they actually go around in a perpetual cycle. Growth will be like that for us. We may seem to ascend at times and descend at others, but for the rest of our lives the cycle won't end (though it draws us closer to God).

We need strength for this lifelong journey. Sometimes, our need for strength takes us completely by surprise.

I remember watching a youth soccer game some years ago. When the opposing team scored against our goalie, someone hollered, "Get that kid out of the goal!" I winced inside, but said nothing. When our team fell another point behind and the stands erupted with "He's no goalie! Get him outta there!" I quietly endured. I even stayed strong while hushed questions drifted through the stands: "What's wrong with that kid's arm?" "Why is his hand fisted like that?" "Do they even allow kids like that into this league?"

But when my bright-eyed, curly-headed five-year-old son raced off the pee-wee soccer field excitedly calling, "Hey Mom, Mom . . . did you see? . . . They let me play goalie . . . and did you see me stop the ball?" my strength gave way. I just couldn't contain my tears.

Do you ever have moments like that? Moments when the bruises of this world wear you down and steal your strength? Moments where you just can't hold it together? We all do, or we wouldn't be here. Rest assured: Strength, too, is found within these Fortress walls. King David knew well this truth:

> For you have been my refuge, a strong tower against the foe. (Psalm 61:3)

> The God of Israel gives power and strength to his people. (Psalm 68:35)

Strength is a common theme in the Bible. In fact, the Scriptures (NIV) mention strength and its closely related idea of power in more than four hundred verses. When I studied these passages, I discovered that both ideas seem to fall into one of two categories: either human-centered strength or God-centered strength. These two have little in common, and only one is found in the Fortress of God. Let's first look at the one with which we are, no doubt, most familiar.

MAN-CENTERED STRENGTH

When I sat in the bleachers that day, trying to stay strong for my soccer-playing son, I relied on human-centered strength. I steeled my emotions. I resolved not to cry. I thought about other things in an attempt at distraction. I even minimized my heartache *(So what if Dan isn't a good goalie . . . This is no big deal)*. Human-centered strength avoids the appearance of weakness: It sheds no tears; it rarely admits struggle; it shows little heartache. It produces a "stiff upper lip" marked by undaunted stoicism.

In the Bible, human-centered strength is characterized this way:

- Human-centered strength relies on self (Deuteronomy 8:17).
- Human-centered strength uses visible, external resources such as wealth, position, influence, possessions, talents, and abilities (Isaiah 31:1).
- Human-centered strength is short-lived (Isaiah 44:12).
- Human-centered strength bears no lasting fruit (Jeremiah 17:5–6).

GOD-CENTERED STRENGTH

God-centered strength is something quite different.

A more God-centered approach to that difficult soccer afternoon would have been to look to God for strength. I could have been honest with God about my heartache. I could have allowed myself to cry (even Jesus wept) without shame. I could have asked for the power to resist hating the rude catcallers who demeaned my handicapped son. I might even have looked to God's goodness and trusted Him with whatever He was doing on that soccer field.

God-centered strength necessarily lifts our eyes from our heartaches and weariness to something beyond ourselves. It is far more effective than any human-centered imitation we might attempt to rely on. Consider:

- God-centered strength *relies on God* (Psalm 18:32).
- God-centered strength *uses unseen, internal resources,* including prayer, the Holy Spirit, quietness, trust, and hope (Isaiah 30:15; 40:31).
- God-centered strength *is eternal* (Psalm 73:26).
- God-centered strength *results in long-term endurance and lasting fruit* (Psalm 84:5–7; Habakkuk 3:19; Colossians 1:10–11).

You see, God-centered strength has nothing to do with "grin and bear it" attitudes, "praise the Lord" flippancy, or pick-yourself-up-by-your-bootstraps determination. It is not absence of feelings or steely resolve. Rather, the strength that comes from God comes only when we honestly admit our weakness to Him. Therein lies its glory.

Listen to the words of Isaiah:

Do you not know? Have you not heard? The LORD is the everlasting God, the Creator of the ends of the earth. He will not grow tired or weary, and his understanding no one can fathom. He gives strength to the weary and increases the power of the weak. (Isaiah 40:28–29)

Did you hear? God gives strength to the *weary*—not the strong, the proud, the determined or steel-hearted. He gives power to the *weak*—not the tough, the bold, the stoic or the self-sure. Recognizing and admitting our weakness is prerequisite for experiencing God's strength.

ADMITTING THAT WE ARE WEAK

The trouble for us is that weakness has little place in our world. Advertisements entice us to take power walks, catch power naps, drink power shakes, and consume power vitamins. They beckon us to put on power makeup, wear power suits, attend power talks, and do power lunches. Why? Because we live in a culture obsessed with power. Power, we reason, is rooted in strength. And if we're to be people of power and influence in our world we must be inherently strong. There is no room for weakness. Yet nothing could be further from the biblical truth.

In 1 Corinthians we read that the body is sown in weakness but raised in power (1 Corinthians 15:43). In Hebrews we hear that the ancient heroes of the faith had weakness turned to strength (Hebrews 11:34). Perhaps the most telling passage on this relationship between weakness and strength is found in 2 Corinthians 12:7–10:

> To keep me from becoming conceited because of these surpassingly great revelations, there was given me a thorn in my flesh, a messenger of Satan, to torment me. Three times I pleaded with the Lord to take it away from me. But he said to me, "My grace is sufficient for you, for my power is made perfect in weakness." Therefore I will boast all the more gladly about my weaknesses, so that Christ's power may rest on me. That is why, for Christ's sake, I delight in weaknesses, in insults, in hardships, in persecutions, in difficulties. For when I am weak, then I am strong.

Some commentators suggest that Paul's "thorn" was a physical impairment. Others say that it was a chronic disease. Still others suggest that it was the ongoing persecution Paul experienced as a result of his preaching. Though the Bible isn't clear about the specifics of Paul's "thorn," it is clear about its purpose: to keep Paul from "becoming conceited." In other words, Paul was given a thorn to keep Him "weak" and reliant on God.

You see, when we admit our weakness and rely on God's strength, God's glory can be revealed (1 Corinthians 2:3–5). When we stop relying on our man-centered resources, we discover God's Tower of Strength.

THE ROLE OF THE FORTRESS TOWERS

A medieval castle's towers served many functions, the most important of which was to strengthen and defend the curtain wall. Towers stood at the fortress's corners, near the gate, and at regular intervals along the walls. In some cases, towers were spaced widely apart, and in others, built closer together. Some towers were round, some angular, some square—each designed to suit its position and role when the castle came under attack.

The towers worked with the keep to strengthen the defense and security of the fortress. The towers did not work alone.

God's Tower of Strength, which surrounds the Staircase of Growth, works similarly. When we admit our weakness, God gives us strength, but that strength works in conjunction with other parts of the Fortress. It is tailored to suit our need:

- When we need comfort, the Tower of Strength and Curtain Wall of Comfort work together to strengthen our sense of God's presence.

- When we're tempted to doubt God's character, the Tower of Strength works with the Keep of Shelter to shore up our faith in God.

- When we fall into sin, the Tower of Strength reinforces the Staircase of Growth, and gives us strength to repent and take the next step.

- When we thirst for renewal, the Tower enables us to pick up the cup and drink from the Well.

When we seek refuge in God's Mighty Fortress, we discover strength in the Tower. That strength works with the rest of the Fortress to secure our refuge. God tailors the strength He provides to our weakness and need.

FINDING STRENGTH IN WEAKNESS

What does this God-centered strength look like? It's strength that works through our weakness—and His strength. The Bible describes it as:

- Continuing the race even in weariness (Isaiah 40:29).
- Not wavering in faith despite impossible odds (Romans 4:19–21).
- Having confidence in prayer when we don't know how to pray (Romans 8:26).
- Recognizing our inability so God's glory will be revealed (1 Corinthians 2:3).
- Taking God's way out when we're weak in temptation (1 Corinthians 10:13).
- Being patient and steadfast when it's tough to endure (Colossians 1:11).
- Not being swayed by false teaching (Hebrews 13:9).

Each of these illustrates a kind of strength that God provides for specific situations. Perhaps the best illustration of God's strength for our spiritual battles is found in Ephesians 6:10–17:

> Finally, be strong in the Lord and in his mighty power. Put on the full armor of God . . . so that when the day of evil comes, you may be able to stand your ground, and after you have done everything, to stand. Stand firm then, with the belt of truth buckled around your waist, with the breastplate of righteousness in place, and with your feet fitted with the readiness that comes from the gospel of peace. In addition to all this, take up the shield of faith, with which you can

extinguish all the flaming arrows of the evil one. Take the helmet of salvation and the sword of the Spirit, which is the word of God.

Can you imagine a knight going into battle wearing only his tunic? How about entering a joust with only a shield? Can you see him trying to rescue a fair maiden using his helmet? How foolish that would be! You see, God doesn't give us strength in isolation. Rather, God's strength flows from the whole of His character. We appropriate His strength by wearing *all* the armor He provides: truth, righteousness, faith, salvation, the Spirit, and the Word of God. The more we put on the *whole* armor of God, the more we experience His strength. But only as we recognize our weakness.

The wonder of weakness is that it is the very thing that allows us to experience God's strength. When we know our need and cry out for help, God gives us His strength. As popular pastor and author Chuck Swindoll noted, "God does not dispense strength and encouragement like a druggist fills your prescription. . . . He promises us Himself. That is all. And that is enough."[1]

The strength God provides comes from His Person. He gives that part of Himself that best suits your need. When facing weakness, if you seek refuge in God and bring your weakness to Him, you will experience the aspect of God you need most. This, too, is an experience of refuge.

-<- PUTTING IT INTO PRACTICE ->>

The danger of human-centered strength—other than denying God's strength—is that it may be symptomatic of a deeper issue: Human-centered strength is often rooted in human-centered faith. Using Table 1 below, prayerfully determine which faith most typifies your walk with God. (Warning: We will all see ourselves on both sides of the table.)

HUMAN-CENTERED FAITH	GOD-CENTERED FAITH
"People will be lovers of themselves …having a form of godliness but denying its power." (2 Timothy 3:2–5)	*Those who hope in the LORD will renew their strength. They will soar on wings like eagles; they will run and not grow weary, they will walk and not be faint."* (Isaiah 40:31)
Lives out of *own strength.*	Lives out of *reliance on God.*
Seeks to *satisfy self.*	Seeks to *please God.*
SELF is *final authority* (picks and chooses what commands to obey).	GOD'S WORD is *final authority* (submits to God's commands).
Faith is rooted in *feelings.*	Faith is rooted in *truth.*
Trusts in *understanding.*	Trusts in *the character of God.*
Has *temporal mind-set.*	Has an *eternal mind-set.*
Believes Christian growth *comes naturally.*	Knows Christian growth *takes grace, effort, perseverance, and endurance.*
Relationship with God focuses *externally.*	Relationship with God focuses *internally* and bears external fruit.
Believes God's primary concern is that I be *happy and comfortable.*	Believes God's primary concern is that I *love Him and become Christlike.*
Forgets to thank God in all circumstances.	Has a *grateful heart* that gives thanks in all circumstances.

Questions for Reflection

1. In which area do you feel weakest right now? Be honest.

2. When you feel weak, do you tend to rely more on human-centered or God-centered strength and power?

3. How can weakness be a good thing in our walks with God?

4. How does our willingness to admit weakness impact our experience of refuge?

5. In your journey through the Mighty Fortress of God so far, which room or structure has helped you the most? Why?

Note

1. Charles Swindoll, *Encourage Me* (Grand Rapids: Zondervan, 1982), 43.

10

I CAN SEE CLEARLY:
The Parapet of Eternal Perspective

But in this [Castle] everything is different. Our good
God now desires to remove the scales from the eyes
of the soul, so that it may see and understand.

TERESA OF AVILA
Interior Castle

⇢⊱⊰⇠

Open my eyes that I may see.

—PSALM 119:18

So we fix our eyes not on what is seen, but on what is unseen.
For what is seen is temporary, but what is unseen is eternal.

—2 CORINTHIANS 4:18

OK, I'll admit it. I'm not terribly adept at finding my way around strange cities. My husband, Don, teases me about my impaired sense of direction. Follow-his-nose-anywhere Donald just doesn't understand how I miss turnpike exits and interstate ramps. Just last weekend, coming home from a speaking engagement in Maryland, I didn't realize I'd missed my turnoff until I drove past the Philadelphia International Airport (which, to my credit, I knew was much farther east than I wanted to be). Sometimes, it seems like I could get lost in a revolving door!

Paris, however, gave me every reason to be directionally impaired. Though I easily navigated her excellent, easy-to-understand underground rail system (called Le Metro), I consistently had difficulty with her city streets. The crowded avenues and café-lined alleyways created a disjointed web of cockeyed passages having no apparent rhyme or reason. I found myself regularly making many wrong turns because I couldn't see how the roads fit together.

That is, until I stood atop the Eiffel Tower.

From the viewing gallery on the tower's third level, nearly nine hundred feet above the ground, I had a completely different view of the streets below. To the north I saw the Arc de Triomphe, a massive stone arch built to commemorate Napoleon's military prowess. Much to my surprise, this massive monument served as the hub of twelve radiating avenues, including the famous Champs Élysées. And—surprise, surprise—it wasn't the only monument to do so. This hub-and-spoke street design connected streets throughout the city. No wonder their layout made no sense me; Parisian streets were a hodgepodge of overlapping wagon wheels all meshed together!

Viewed at eye level, they were a jumbled mess, but my bird's-eye view provided a clearer picture.

Life is like that, isn't it? We often find ourselves immersed in what appears to be a tangled net of circumstances that, when viewed through human eyes, leaves us disoriented and confused. But, as we begin to see our circumstances through the lens of the eternal, our vision clears.

THE VIEW FROM THE PARAPET

Welcome to the Parapet of Eternal Perspective! You've climbed the Staircase of Growth and found strength in the Tower, and now you've emerged high atop the castle walls. The Parapet provides a welcome place to stroll far above the castle grounds.

The parapet lined the very top of a castle's walls and towers. It provided a walkway around the perimeter of the highest regions of the fortress. Because of its clear, unobstructed view, castle guards used the parapet to survey surrounding lands for game, approaching storms, or advancing enemies. From here, like the guards, you see things differently.

We all face challenging circumstances, and whether we know it or not, we view those circumstances through some kind of lens: the lens of past experience, the lens of feelings, the lens of human understanding, the lens of priorities or values. We all wear glasses of sorts, and we look at the world and what happens to us through those glasses. The apostle Paul faced some pretty confusing circumstances, too, but he viewed them through the lens of God's purposes. Listen to how he describes them: "We do not want you to be uninformed, brothers, about the hardships we suffered in the province of Asia. We were under great pressure, far beyond our ability to endure, so that we despaired even of life. Indeed, in our hearts we felt the sentence of death" (2 Corinthians 1:8–9).

Paul's circumstances were so difficult that he despaired even of life. Biblical scholars suggest that the suffering he refers to in this passage may have included imprisonment and beatings (1 Corinthians 15:32), a riot, and an attempt on his life in Ephesus (Acts 19:23–41), or a severe attack of some recurring sickness. The details aren't clear in the text, but one thing is certain: These events caused Paul great distress. When viewed through the temporal lens of a finite world, suffering like his could easily result in despair.

But Paul didn't stay in despair. He concluded, "But this happened that we might not rely on ourselves but on God" (2 Corinthians 1:9). Paul understood that there was another way to view his circumstances: through the lens of God's higher ways.

You've come to the place in your refuge journey where you now stand far above the Bailey. Did you notice the view from up here? The view from the Parapet sheds different light on the surrounding terrain of your circumstances. What difficulties do you face just now? Through what lens do you view them? Has your view changed since you entered the Fortress?

THE LONG-RANGE PERSPECTIVE

Several years ago, we had the delightful opportunity to hike in the French Alps. My husband and I are both hikers; our children are not. Like all novice hikers, they enjoyed the first part of our trek. The terrain was easy, interesting, and new. But, as the trail got steeper and the path more difficult, the kids grew weary and impatient. Putting one foot in front of the other, they ascended slowly without being able to see the summit. The destination was too remote and the climb too painstaking for their instant-gratification minds. The going was hard, and they wanted to quit.

Don and I had a different perspective. We'd read the map; we knew what to expect; we knew there was an end in sight. We also knew that the panoramic view from the summit would be well worth the climb. Because the kids didn't share our perspective, their ascent was arduous. Because we had a larger view, we enjoyed the climb.

As Christians, we often look at life the same way my kids viewed our hike in the Alps—a series of uphill, purposeless battles with no end in sight. We get tired, discouraged, and want to give up. Our weariness drives us to seek refuge. What we find in God's refuge again surprises us: *Refuge doesn't change our circumstances; it changes us.* We discover a different perspective—the higher perspective of the Lord of the Fortress.

One of the greatest benefits of seeking refuge in God is that the nearer we draw to the Lord of the Fortress, the more we begin to see our world from His perspective.

GOD'S GREAT PERSPECTIVE

How does God's perspective differ from ours?

1. *God's ways are not our ways.* Don't be surprised if God's ways don't seem to make sense. His perspective will seem foreign. Scripture tells us that "[God's] thoughts are not [our] thoughts" (Isaiah 55:8), and that the wisdom of God is foolishness to men (1 Corinthians 1:18–25). Proverbs warns us not to lean on our own understanding (Proverbs 3:5). We may not understand what God is doing or why, just as our kids didn't understand why we hiked the route we did, but as we discovered in the Keep, we can trust Him.

2. *God has an end in mind.* As a child, I remember my wise Uncle Luther giving us a lesson one July day on his Christmas tree farm. It was tree-trimming time, and I listened in as he instructed my older cousins, who were summer workers there. "Christmas trees don't just become Christmas trees, you know. You've got to see the final shape of the tree, then cut the cross-growing branches."

   Sounds a bit like how God shapes us, doesn't it? God knows the desired shape of our lives (He wants us to love Him and be holy). He will cut the limbs growing in opposition to His desired result. (In other words, He prunes us.) And, yes, He will bring circumstances into our lives to accomplish that end. When we begin to view our circumstances through the lens of God's desired ends, we begin to see our challenges in a different light. They become God's means of shaping us into the people He wants us to be. Rather than resisting His

126

work in us, we can yield to His molding.

3. *God's perspective is eternal.* It's all too easy for us to focus on the here and now, but this life is only temporary. God, however, is eternal. He sees the beginning from the end and works all things to achieve His end. Let us, like Jesus, fix our eyes squarely on the unseen eternal purposes of God (Hebrews 12:2). Then we will be able to say with Paul, "Therefore we do not lose heart. . . . For our light and momentary troubles are achieving for us an eternal glory that far outweighs them all. So we fix our eyes not on what is seen, but on what is unseen. For what is seen is temporary, but what is unseen is eternal" (2 Corinthians 4:16–18).

DEVELOPING ETERNAL PERSPECTIVE

So how do we learn to view our lives and circumstances from the Parapet of Eternal Perspective? In part, we already know how. The farther we traveled into this Mighty Fortress, the more we learned about the nature and ways of God. The closer we move to Him, the more we begin to see things His way. Learning about God's person and purposes clears our vision and gives us an eye for the eternal.

We can also try these concrete steps to view our troubles through the lens of eternity:

1. *Ask "what?" not "why?"* In times of needing refuge, we are often tempted to ask the age-old question, "Why?" We would do well to remember that almighty God, the Creator of the universe, owes us no answers. When Job, who never lost faith, persisted in questioning God, God never answered the questions Job raised. God did, however, reveal Himself to Job, and that was enough. Instead of asking God "Why?" we can develop eternal perspective by asking, "What do you want me learn through this, Lord?"

2. *View our circumstances through the lens of God's character, not vice versa.* In other words, we can't allow our circumstances to

distort our perception of God. Well-known author and speaker Barbara Johnson almost lost her husband in a near-fatal automobile accident. While her husband was still recovering, not one but two grown sons met tragic deaths (the first in Vietnam and, five years later, the other by a drunk driver). Two years after the second funeral, she lost a third son to the homosexual lifestyle. (He later returned.) This hurting mother could have chosen to let her circumstances alter her perception of God. Instead, she viewed her circumstances through the lens of the God that demonstrated His love for her on the cross. She came to a place of "Whatever, Lord,"[1] surrendering all her pain and heartache to a good, trustworthy, sovereign God who was accomplishing His plan.

3. *Study the purposes of God.* Using a concordance, topical Bible, or the index in the back of your Bible, look up words or phrases that might help you discover God's purposes: "purpose(s)," "plan(s)," "please(s)," "desire(s)," "way(s)," "will," or any variant of "eternal." As you read these passages, you will begin to see what is important to God. Knowing what is important to God helps us develop the higher perspective of His eternal purposes.

4. *Think about eternity.* How often in our whirlwind lives do we stop and think about the life to come? Truth be told, what we call eternity, our eternal life with God, is actually more "real" than present-day "reality." This life is but a blip on the eternal screen of time. Take a moment in the course of your day to stop, close your eyes, and think about eternity.

Of these four steps, the last one may be the hardest. Thinking about eternity in a world caught in the here and now is not easy. Sometimes schedules and even well-meaning friends make us think the present and the urgent are more important. So how do you pause in the course of a day and think about eternity? Here are five questions for you to contemplate—questions that are bound to put your mind on eternity with God:

• What will it be like to live in God's tangible presence, seeing Him face-to-face every day?

- What will it be like to live in a world rid of sorrow, suffering, pain, and tears?
- How will it feel to see your Savior, your Bridegroom, your Lord?
- How will it feel to be free of sin (both our own and that of others)?
- How will it feel to have God curl His finger under your chin, lift your head, and with eyes brightly shining, say, "Well done, good and faithful servant"?

IT'S COMING!

Can you feel the longing? Do you sense the joy? Eternity is real and it's coming. It won't be long now. Embrace the eternal; it may change your here and now.

One last note: The Parapet of Eternal Perspective is a welcome place, but it can be unnerving. As noted, it takes a while to adjust to standing this far above the maddening distractions of the busy world below. Be patient. Developing eternal perspective takes time. It's more than answering a series of questions, of course. It's a process that is wholly dependent on our progress through the Fortress.

The deeper you go, and the more you walk these heights, the more fitting this perspective will feel. We were, after all, designed for eternity. We have but to avail ourselves to God's eternal purposes and we will begin to see things through His eyes.

⊰ PUTTING IT INTO PRACTICE ⊱

On a piece of paper, write down the circumstance in which you most need refuge. As you look at what you have written, pray and ask God these questions:

1. What are you trying to accomplish, Lord, both in and through me?
2. How can I better honor You in this circumstance?
3. What is most important to You in this situation?

Quietly reflect on the answers God gives you and record them on your paper. Then ask yourself, "How might I view this circumstance differently in a month, six months, a year, five years, and at the end of my life?"

Questions for Reflection

1. Have your circumstances ever been so difficult that you despaired even of life? Explain.

2. Read 2 Corinthians 1:8–10. What was the purpose of Paul's suffering? What was his hope?

3. Read 2 Corinthians 4:16–18. How does this passage encourage you to view your struggles?

4. How might God's ways be different than ours?

5. What one step can you take to develop more of an eternal perspective?

Note

1. Barbara Johnson, *The Best of Barbara Johnson* (New York: Inspirational Press, 1996), 57.

11

MORE THAN JUST WISHING:
The Banner of Hope

Hope is inseparable from faith in the true God.

REBECCA MANLEY PIPPERT
A Heart Like His

Yet this I call to mind and therefore I have hope:
Because of the LORD's great love we are not consumed.

—LAMENTATIONS 3:21–22

Let us hold unswervingly to the hope we profess,
for he who promised is faithful.

—HEBREWS 10:23

When I was a little girl, I had all kinds of hopes. I hoped for a "Nancy Nurse" doll. I hoped for a two-wheeler bike with a banana seat, spider handlebars, and grips with multi-colored streamers (this was the 1960s, remember). I hoped to attend camp in the summer and to visit my uncle's farm at Thanksgiving. I even hoped that the tooth fairy would come.

The summer after second grade, I hoped for a puppy. My twin sister and I begged and pleaded, and our hopes increased exponentially when Mom finally caved with "Well, maybe. But, *if* we get a puppy, it has to be a male, it has to be housebroken, and it can't cost more than a dollar." "Maybe" meant "yes" as far as we were concerned.

But weeks passed without a hint of a puppy. Our July birthday came and went. Summer turned to fall, school started, leaves began dropping, and there was still no sign that our hope would be satisfied. Over time our puppy longing waned and we soon forgot that we'd hoped at all.

With the crisp October air came our town's annual library auction. The auction was a small affair boasting tent-covered tables of used books for sale, a few scattered food booths, and an auction platform complete with auctioneer, bullhorn, and donated items to be sold to the highest bidder. My sister and I thought the auction was boring, but the funnel cakes were good, so we tagged along with our bargain-hunting dad.

The autumn eve soon turned bone-chilling: The funnel cakes were cold and the canvas tents dripped with rain. We wanted to go home, but Dad wasn't ready.

"There's something I'm waiting to bid on," he explained, a twinkle in his eye. "Look there."

At first, my sister and I saw nothing of interest on the platform. Then someone handed a big, open-topped cardboard carton to the auctioneer. *Great, another box of junk,* we thought. But our disinterest turned to curiosity, which turned to hope-filled excitement when the auctioneer pulled out a squirming, whimpering ball of copper-colored fur.

It was a puppy! Our forgotten hope. Our dream. Was this what Dad had been waiting for?

"Do I have twenty-five cents for this lovable, Heinz-fifty-seven variety?" the auctioneer called into his ringing bullhorn while holding the quivering pup in the air.

"Daddy, Daddy, pleeeeeeeeasse?" my sister and I chorused.

"Remember what your mother said? 'Only a housebroken male.' That puppy's a female and she can't be more than six weeks old." He shook his head.

"But we'll take care of it. We'll teach it to go outside. We'll clean up after it every day. Please, please, pretty pleeeeease?"

Dad looked at our hope-filled faces, and raised his hand. "I'll bid twenty-five cents."

"I hear twenty-five, twenty-five, twenty-five, twenty-five," the auctioneer called. "I have twenty-five; do I hear fifty?"

Much to our dismay an overalls-clad man in the corner raised his hand.

"I hear fifty. How about seventy-five?" We tugged on Dad's trouser leg and looked up with four pleading eyes. Dad raised his hand again.

The man in the denim overalls bid one dollar.

We held our breath when the caller pointed at Dad and asked "Will you go two?" Mom had said "no more than a dollar." What would Dad do? Dad looked at us, then looked at the puppy, then back at us again.

"One-fifty," he nodded. Our hopes soared.

Our hopes seesawed over the next several minutes. Dad and the man in the overalls continued their contest; one would bid, the other would counter. At four dollars, Dad wavered, and the bidding slowed. Four-ten. Four-twenty. Back and forth the two men went, until it was Dad's turn to bid five.

"I have four-ninety, four-ninety, four-ninety, four ninety. Will you go five?" Dad hesitated. Five dollars in 1967 was a lot of money, especially for a mutt.

"Four-ninety going once."

No! That other man was going to get our puppy!

"Daddy, please!" We jumped up and down and pulled on his arms.

"Four ninety going twice."

"Daaaaaaadddeeeeeeeee!" we begged. He tilted his head and sighed. Five dollars was just too much. Our hopes crashed. Dad had tried, but the cost was too great.

"Sssssooool . . ." we heard the caller begin.

"Five dollars!" Dad interrupted with finality. The man in the corner shrugged his shoulders, shook his head, turned, and walked away.

"SOLD for five dollars to the gentleman with the twins." My sister and I squealed, hugged each other, hugged Dad, and sprinted for the platform. The precious puppy was ours! Now we just had to tell Mom that the housebroken-less-than-a-dollar-male puppy she'd ordered was an untrained, six-week-old female who'd broken the bank.

HOPE: POSSIBILITIES AND CERTAINTIES

There's nothing quite like hope. We see it all around us. We see hope in the eyes of a child waking up Christmas morning; in the demeanor of a recent grad starting his first real job; in the glow of a wife announcing she's pregnant; in the gaze of an engaged couple who just set "the date." We feel hopeful with the dawn of a new day or when the sun pierces a storm-filled sky. We see it in the farmer who sows, the fisherman who casts, the bird-watcher who waits, and the sea captain who scans the horizon for shore. Though none is guaranteed an end result, all wait expectantly. All look forward to a possibility hoped for, but not ensured.

That kind of hope—a positive, expectant view toward the future—is what we often mean when we use the word "hope." It's like wishful thinking. We look forward with longing toward a possible, though not guaranteed, end. That hope deals in *possibilities*—the things that *might* be.

Biblical hope is different. Though the longing is similar, true biblical hope deals with *certainties*—with the things that *will* be. That's the kind of hope Simeon had.

A MAN OF HOPE

We read about Simeon in Luke 2:25–35. Simeon was a righteous and devout Jew who longed for the "consolation of Israel" (Luke 2:25). He looked for the comfort that would come with the advent of the promised Messiah. Early in his life, the Holy Spirit revealed to Simeon that he would not die before seeing the promised Savior (verse 26). Year after year, decade after decade, Simeon waited for God's promise to be fulfilled. By the time Jesus was born, Simeon was old and still waiting for the Savior. Can you imagine what the waiting was like for him? And yet he continued to hope, certain of God's promise.

We read that the Spirit prompted Simeon, now well into his golden years, to go to the temple courts. How many times had he gone before? How many times had his prayers seemed unanswered? But one more time he went. Can you imagine him scanning the crowd, taking note of each couple bringing a child to be consecrated to God? You can almost feel his pulse quicken as he looked for *the* child, the one who would become the Hope of Israel. Though his old eyes had yet to see the Savior, his hope lived on. After a lifetime of searching, he searched still.

This time it was different. In a temple court in Jerusalem, Simeon saw what he'd been promised long ago. His heart quickened and he knew.

> When the parents brought in the child Jesus to do for him what the custom of the Law required, Simeon took him in his arms and praised God, saying: "Sovereign Lord, as you have promised, you now dismiss your servant in peace. For my eyes have seen your salvation, which you have prepared in the sight of all people, a light for revelation to the Gentiles and for glory to your people Israel." (Luke 2:27–32)

Simeon spent a lifetime hoping in God's promise. His was a biblical hope—one grounded on the *certainty* of what God had said He would do. But it wasn't until the very end of his life that God allowed Simeon to see hope fulfilled. Simeon lived by a hope unseen, and yet persevered. How?

HOPE AND FAITH TOGETHER

I think the key is found in Luke 2:25, which describes Simeon as a "righteous and devout" man. Simeon was a man of faith. Like a dual-oxen team, biblical hope and faith work together; you cannot have one without the other. To have faith is to hope (certain of God's promise) and to hope is to have faith. As A. W. Tozer noted, "Faith is the gaze of a soul upon a saving God."[1]

Biblically, faith is hope applied; it is being sure of something hoped for but not realized. Hebrews 11:1 defines faith this way: "Faith is being sure of what we hope for and certain of what we do not see." After giving this definition of faith, the writer of Hebrews describes faith-filled men and women of the past: Abel, Enoch, Noah, Abraham, Isaac, Jacob, Joseph, Moses, etc. But the writer doesn't stop with these heroes. He continues with those who had a different experience and outcome:

> Others were tortured. . . . Some faced jeers and flogging, while still others were chained and put in prison. They were stoned; they were sawed in two; they were put to death by the sword. They went about in sheepskins and goatskins, destitute, persecuted and mistreated— the world was not worthy of them. They wandered in deserts and mountains, and in caves and holes in the ground. (Hebrews 11:35–38)

Yet, the passage continues, "These were all commended for their faith, yet none of them received what had been promised" (Hebrews 11:39). These suffering men and women are given as examples of faith, though they didn't see miracles and though they didn't live to see the fulfillment of their hope. Unlike Simeon, they died before the promised end occurred.

These saints of old found hope not in their circumstances but in the *certainty* that God's promise would be fulfilled. They were confident, though they didn't see it happen, that God would do what He said He would do.

A BANNER OF CONFIDENCE

They weren't the only men and women of the past who knew what it meant to have confidence. Medieval castle dwellers did, too.

Castle dwellers felt confident whenever they gazed at the banner flying high above the castle's towers. (Well, if they dwelled in the fortress of a *good* and *capable* king, they had confidence—the banner of a tyrant would elicit a completely different response.) The castle's banner displayed the lord's crest and, much like today's national flags, it signified who owned and ruled the castle. The specific symbols on the banner testified to something about the lord himself: Perhaps he was known for military prowess or for his passion for knowledge; he may have been a man of faith or widespread esteem. The symbols reflected their lord and him alone.

The banner reminded castle dwellers of their lord, the one in whom they'd placed their hope for justice, defense, provision, freedom, and well-being. Their confidence wasn't in the banner itself, but in the man behind the banner. When castle dwellers viewed the banner waving above the fortress, it assured them of the certainty of their lord's reign and of his character and cause. Hope was found in their king.

"The LORD is my Banner," we read in the Old Testament (Exodus 17:15). This name was first used in Scripture when God defended His people, Israel, from attacking Amalekites. During the battle, Moses (the leader of the Israelites), his brother Aaron, and another Israelite leader, Hur, stood atop a hill overlooking the battle. As long as Moses kept his arms raised in petition to almighty God, the battle tipped in favor of Israel. If he lowered his arms, the Amalakites would succeed. Aaron and Hur helped Moses keep his arms lifted to God for the battle's duration, and Israel won. Moses built an altar in recognition of God as his "Banner."

Banner, in this context, meant recognizing that the battle belonged to God and that the victory was His and His alone. Israel's hope for victory was found in God's person, power, and plan. Our hope, like theirs, is in Him (Psalm 71:5).

CONFIDENCE IN THE LORD OF THE FORTRESS

We've learned much about God in our journey so far. In the outer regions of the Fortress, we found that God is a giving God who does many good things. In the middle regions, we learned more of who God is—good, trustworthy, sovereign, holy, etc.—and started viewing our lives and circumstances from His perspective. The farther we move into the Fortress, the more certain we become of God and His Word. When we develop confidence in the Lord of this Fortress, new, biblical hope is born (or kindled anew).

It's amazing how confidence in God changes things:

When we entered the gatehouse, we thought, *Can God even be trusted? Yes,* our hearts cry now from above.

When our burdens grew weighty, we wondered, *Does God even care? More than we know,* we can affirm with relief.

When we needed comfort, we questioned, *Is God even here? Surrounding always,* we know now and believe.

Through each room or structure we cried out for some new understanding, and God answered us with Himself or His Word. As Paul told the Romans, "For everything that was written in the past was written to teach us, so that through endurance and the encouragement of the Scriptures we might have hope" (Romans 15:4). In every region of our castle journey, the Scriptures pointed us to the certainty that God is who He claims to be and will do what He has promised. Our confidence has grown, and now we can hope.

Does biblical hope mean that we are certain we will get what we want (like banana bikes and puppies at auctions)? Does it mean our longings will be fulfilled in this life? Does it mean we'll get the job, get the husband (or wife), get the check, or the recognition we want? No. Biblical hope doesn't grant wishes or guarantee satisfaction of our wants.

Hope, like eternal perspective, is set on the promises of God and on His ability to keep those promises. It's more than positive feeling or expectant desire; it is a resolute attitude of heart that knows that God will do what He has said He will do.

It is also an "already, but not yet" experience. Yes, Jesus is our hope, and we already have His promised salvation, but we look forward expectantly to His return. Yes, our hope for eternity with God is guaranteed, but we long for the day when we'll meet Him face-to-face. Hope, in this life, means that, though we've already had our hope fulfilled in part, we look forward expectantly, and perhaps longingly, to its complete fulfillment. It's a waiting marked with certainty.

HOW DO WE FOSTER HOPE?

We don't foster biblical hope by doing what I did while I waited for a puppy. Hoping for a puppy was wishful-thinking hope; it wasn't grounded on certainty. Over those summer months when the puppy didn't come, I just gave up. I was disappointed, and when my answer didn't come soon enough, I quit hoping. I forgot the desire of my heart. Little did my young mind know that my parents had a plan and were working it out even while my hope dwindled.

To foster biblical hope, the hope marked with certainty, remember the lessons of the Fortress so far. Remember that God is there and that He is good. Remember that He is sovereign and has an eternal end in mind. Remember what Paul taught in Romans 5:3–5: "We also rejoice in our sufferings [in this case, fulfillment deferred], because we know that suffering produces perseverance; perseverance, character; and character, hope. And hope does not disappoint us, because God has poured out his love into our hearts by the Holy Spirit, whom he has given us."

Look at the Banner of Hope; be reminded of the Lord of the Banner. As you gaze at Him and remember that the battle is His, and the victory is assured, your hope will be renewed.

⊰⊹ PUTTING IT INTO PRACTICE ⊹⊱

If you happen to be one of those visual, artistic types, take a moment to sketch a banner that reflects the mighty Lord of this Fortress. Think about the God behind the banner while you sketch. Is your hope in Him?

If you are not artistic by nature, just visualize what the banner of God's Fortress might look like. Make a list of what you might include on the banner. You might include images like scales of justice, a heart of love, a light of truth, or a sun on the horizon. You may also include a tree of life, a shepherd's crook, a king's crown, or a potter's wheel. The Bible is full of images describing God. Which would you include on your banner?

Hang your banner or your list in a place where you are likely to see it often. When you are tempted to give up, when your circumstances feel hopeless, look at your banner and remember the Lord of the Fortress.

Questions for Reflection

1. Do you identify with Simeon's waiting? In what ways?

2. Is your hope grounded on possibilities (wishful thinking) or certainties (biblical truth)?

3. Read Psalm 119:114. What connection do you see between the first part of the verse, "You are my refuge and my shield," and the second part of the verse, "I have put my hope in your word"?

4. From what you've learned in your castle journey so far, upon what can you build your hope?

5. In what way is your hope an "already, but not yet" experience?

Note

1. A. W. Tozer, *The Pursuit of God* (Harrisburg, Pa.: Christian Publications, 1948), 89.

PART THREE

The Innermost Rooms

-+>-<+-

*God can be known in personal experience. A loving Personality
dominates the Bible, walking among the trees of the garden and
breathing fragrance over every scene. Always a living Person is
present, speaking, pleading, loving, working, and manifesting
Himself whenever and wherever His people have the receptivity
necessary to receive the manifestation.*

-+>-<+-

A. W. TOZER
The Pursuit of God

Our journey through the castle's middle regions has been an experience of contrasts. We celebrated God's goodness but ached over our sin. We feared God's holiness but drew closer to Him. We grew in obedience but relied on the Spirit for growth. We experienced God's strength by admitting our weakness. Despite the contrasts, our path through this part of the Fortress led us to deeper refuge. But our journey is not complete.

An even deeper refuge—the deepest of all—waits for us in the rooms ahead. We have simply to move forward with the hope and confidence we discovered in the middle regions. God Himself, the Lord of this Fortress, is drawing us near. Can you hear His call? It's time, now, to journey into the castle's innermost regions where we find our heart's delight and truest refuge for the soul.

12

BETTER THAN HAPPINESS:
The Great Hall of Joy

*Our lives can be lived well, with courage and with joy, because we
live by the hope of the resurrection. So no matter what life lands in
our laps, if we will only trust God and wait . . . the time will come
when faith becomes sight and hope fulfillment and our whole beings
are united with the God we love. Joy of all joys, goal of our desire, all
that we long for will be ours for we will be His.*

REBECCA MANLEY PIPPERT
Hope Has Its Reasons

"No one will take away your joy."

JESUS
John 16:22

–⧓–

But let all who take refuge in you be glad;
let them ever sing for joy.

—PSALM 5:11

The hope we discovered under the Banner of Hope necessarily leads to joy. Even hope unfulfilled. We see this connection in Romans 15:13, where Paul wrote, "May the God of hope fill you with all joy and peace as you trust in him, so that you may overflow with hope by the power of the Holy Spirit." Joy flows from the God of all hope. It comes from His Spirit (who is God) within us. Joy, like hope, is rooted in certainty.

One summer, Don and I had the privilege of teaching at a weeklong conference for pastors and their wives in Kericho, Kenya. I must say that Kenya is beautiful beyond compare: the Masai Mara plain teems with giraffes, wildebeests, elephants, and zebras; the Rift Valley provides dramatic, panoramic views; the Kericho Highlands are lush and green. All are steeped in their own majesty. For all its beauty, however, Kenya was very much a land of disconnects for me.

Kericho may be the world's third largest exporter of tea, but her citizens live in abject poverty. Cell phones abound, but so does malaria. Manicured plantations span rolling hills, but workers live in silos meant for corn. Kenya was full of incongruities, but one incongruity stood out above them all: the people.

Their hospitality and grace moved me to tears. Their collective passion for God encouraged my soul. I was deeply touched by how these dear brothers and sisters in Christ welcomed us not as Americans, but as part of the family of God. But the thing I couldn't get, the disconnect for me, was that these warm, vigorous, hand-shaking Kenyans, despite oppressive, sometimes heartbreaking circumstances, knew that God was who He claimed to be and would do what He had promised to do. Because their hope in Him was certain, they were filled with joy.

JOY IN THE GREAT HALL

Such joy is unlike that found in a medieval fortress. The closest thing to joy in a medieval fortress was found in the castle's Great Hall. This enormous room echoed with music and laughter during wedding banquets, hunting feasts, and royal welcomes. Trumpets gladly sounded each procession of food-bearing servants and gift-bearing travelers. High paneled ceilings resounded with song, while nobles reclined eating their fill.

The lord of the fortress would spare no expense to entertain his honored guests: the best linens, gold or silver plates, soups, aspics, wild game, pies, tarts—these testified to the host's wealth and standing in society. The Great Hall, in all its excess, provided a happy reprieve from the difficulties of everyday life. It was not, however, a place of joy.

The Great Hall to which you've come is different. This is where the medieval image of refuge breaks down. When you sought refuge in God, you didn't enter a medieval castle; you entered His Fortress. You aren't in a medieval banquet room; you stand in the Great Hall of God. More than happiness echoes here; in God's Great Hall joy will fill your soul.

WHAT IS JOY?

Trying to define joy is like trying to squeeze Jell-O. The tighter we grasp it, the more elusive it becomes. When something is difficult to define or understand, it helps to first explore what it is *not*.

Joy is not happiness. In the comic strip *Peanuts,* the Charles Schultz character Charlie Brown used to say, "Happiness is a warm puppy." In some ways, Charlie was right. Happiness is found in things like warm puppies and fuzzy kittens, in hot mugs of cocoa on cold winter days, in lazy summer Sundays on hot sandy beaches, and walks in the park with loved ones or friends. Happiness comes from and depends on what is happening and whom we are with.

Happiness is a positive feeling that results from glad events or satisfying circumstances, but it is not joy. As Philadelphia preacher Donald Grey Barnhouse noted, "Joy must not be confused with mirth; the latter is effervescent, but joy is the steady tenor of our being. When all is chaos on the surface, deep down there is joy."[1]

But knowing what joy is not doesn't define it for us. To better understand joy it may help to look at models of joy.

In 2 Corinthians 8:2 Paul described the Macedonian church: "Out of the most severe trial, their overflowing joy and their extreme poverty welled up in rich generosity." Joy in Macedonia came out of severe hardship.

James wrote, "Consider it pure joy, my brothers, whenever you face trials of many kinds" (James 1:2). For the scattered church in Jerusalem, joy was possible in the midst of suffering and pain.

For Christians in Asia Minor, joy was linked with persecution for their faith and hope for eternity: "But rejoice that you participate in the sufferings of Christ, so that you may be overjoyed when his glory is revealed" (1 Peter 4:13).

In Hebrews we read that Jesus "for the joy set before him endured the cross" (12:2). For Jesus, joy looked forward to the future and made the present bearable.

Biblical joy was not limited to happy times and places; it, in fact, rose out of less-than-happy occasions. What is joy then? The best attempt I can make at defining joy is that it is a *sense of delight flowing from certain hope*. It is both reactive and proactive; it is both feeling and choice. It can well up in emotion, but there is a certainty at its core.

This kind of joy won't be found in comfortable circumstances or superficial faith. As author Paul Tillich stated,

> Eternal joy is not to be reached by living on the surface. It is rather attained by breaking through the surface, by penetrating the deep things of ourselves, of our world, and of God. . . . For in the depth is truth; and in the depth is hope; and in the depth is joy.[2]

The difference between happiness and joy is like the difference between snorkeling and scuba diving. I used to be an avid snorkeler. On a hot summer afternoon, nothing was more relaxing for me than to drift along on a lake's surface viewing fish and plant life below. Snorkeling was rewarding, but it had its limitations. To see anything at all I had to stay close to shore where the water wasn't too deep. Even my view of the underwater habitat was limited; only certain species of fish and plants populate shallow waters. Oh, and on the surface, I was still distracted by the noisy world above.

Scuba diving is completely different; it reveals an entire world unknown to the snorkler. Deeper waters teem with aquatic life unseen from the surface, and one can descend ten, twenty, thirty feet (or more) with oxygen strapped to the back for a close-up look. You can stay submerged for long periods of time, oblivious to surface distractions. Scuba diving moves you from being a passive observer to becoming an active participant in the beauty below. You can't help but become immersed in the quiet wonder of the deep.

Happiness, like snorkeling, is a surface experience. It may give us a taste of what lies beneath the surface, but it is only a taste, nothing more. Joy is found in the depths of our souls when we immerse ourselves in the things of God.

JOY IN THE DEPTHS OF GOD

We find joy when we move beyond the realms of superficial religion. Joy comes as we plumb the deeper things of God. Perhaps this is why our African brothers and sisters know joy so well. Desperate material needs, ongoing tribal wars, relentless persecution, and oppressive pagan belief systems drive them to deeper dependence on God. They have a storm-forged faith that is rare in the comfortable churches of prosperous nations. God is alive to the Kenyan Christians. It is amazing to me how precious Jesus becomes when all else is stripped away.

How does Jesus become more precious to us? How do we move from surface religion to the deep things of God?

- We delight in God's presence (Psalms 16:11; 21:6).

- We allow God Himself to become our joy (Psalms 28:7; 43:4; Isaiah 58:14).

- We reflect on God's Word (Psalms 19:8; 119:111; Jeremiah 15:16).

- We remember our salvation (Psalms 71:23; 95:1; 132:16; Isaiah 12:2–4; Acts 16:34).

- We meditate on our certain future with God (Hebrews 12:2).

- We ponder what God has done (Psalms 92:4; 94:19; 126:3).

- We look forward to what God will do (Isaiah 35:6; 51:3).

- We recall God's victories (Psalms 20:5; 21:1).

- We look for God's work in others (Romans 16:19; Philippians 1:7; 1 Thessalonians 3:9; 2 John 4; 3 John 3).

Look over this list. Does anything seem familiar? Look again. *Every one* of these is found in the Mighty Fortress of God, and *every one* is a biblical source of joy! Our salvation, God's presence, God's Word, remembrance, hope, eternal perspective, expectancy—all have been part of our refuge journey. Joy is found when we take refuge in God (Psalm 5:11).

Do you feel joyless? Are you lacking in joy? Read through and meditate on each of the sources of joy above. Your joy will abound.

THE KEYS TO GREATEST JOY

We've tasted joy in our journey so far, but did you know that your joy can be fuller still? Yes, it's true! Our joy deepens when we recognize our ongoing oneness with our Savior. John 15:5 tells us that "[Jesus is] the vine; [we] are the branches." As a branch is attached to a vine, so we are joined to Him. Did you realize that the Jesus with whom you are joined was full of joy! Yes, joy, and He wants His joy to fill us to the full (John 15:11).

What was this joy that Jesus had? Oswald Chambers wrote, "The joy of Jesus was the absolute self-surrender and self-sacrifice of Himself to His Father, the joy of doing that which the Father sent Him to do."[3] His joy was linked to obedience to His Father's will. His joy flowed from His oneness with the Father and His union of purpose with Him.

Believe it or not, your union with Christ is already an objective reality—now, this moment, even as you read these words! That union began the moment you crossed the Drawbridge of Faith. You became irrevocably united with Him. That's a fact you can count on no matter what you may feel. Do you need proof?

- Have you ever experienced "aha" moments when you read the Bible? The lightbulb goes on in your head and you understand something you never understood before? That's evidence of your union with the Savior and the presence of the Holy Spirit in you. (His Spirit alone reveals truth and applies it to our hearts.)

- Have you ever been surprised by the desire to do something you know pleases God, but that you might have resisted before? There is it again: union with Christ at work. (The desire to please God comes from His work in our hearts.)

- Have you ever found your mind wandering in prayer, but drawn back to God's presence? Your union with Christ brings you back to Him. (God draws us to Himself, even while we pray.)

Think with me for a minute. The almighty God of this Fortress dwells within us. His joy-filled presence fills our souls. Like a child in the womb infused with her mother's life, we are infused with the life of our Father. In Him, we live and move and have our being (Acts 17:28). This life in Christ is not something we have to beg or plead for; it's already ours! Oh, how transformed we would be if we really believed this truth, and how our hearts would overflow with joy!

But we rob ourselves of joy, don't we? We forget that our oneness with Christ is *real* because we don't *feel* Him there. This is where joy becomes proactive; this is where choice comes in. Just as in other realms of the Fortress, here, too, we can choose to believe with certainty that Jesus dwells within and that we are *always* united to Him no matter what our senses tell us. If this is true (and it is), then we can live out that union day to day, moment to moment, just as the branch draws life from the vine (John 15:5).

When we *know*, with certainty, that we, even now, are united to Jesus, our Lord, the tender Lover of our souls, our hearts can't help but to soar with hope and overflow with delight. This is the joy of God's Fortress.

-+ PUTTING IT INTO PRACTICE +-

*Though union with Christ and its resulting joy are
already ours, and though we can never sever that union
(Romans 8:38–39), we can stifle our oneness with Him. Our
life on the vine is stunted when we don't yield to the Spirit
(Galatians 5:16–25) and when we disobey Christ's commands
(John 15:10–11). Yieldedness and obedience are key to experiencing joy.*

*Take a moment now to examine your heart. How yielded
are you to God's ownership? How willing are you to go where
He leads? Are there any areas of disobedience lurking in the
dark corners of your soul? Are there truths from Scripture
that you just aren't willing to believe? Pray and ask God to
forgive you for your unbelief and disobedience. Then ask Him
to give you a heart fully yielded to Him.*

*Now reflect on the sources of joy found on page 151 and
on your oneness with Jesus. Meditate on His presence within
you. Do you sense the joy rising in the depth of your being?
Embrace His joy and let it fill your soul.*

Questions for Reflection

1. How is joy different than happiness? Describe your experience with each.

2. How are hope and joy related?

3. When it comes to the things of God, would you describe yourself as a snorkeler or a scuba diver? Explain.

4. Has your view of oneness with Christ changed since reading this chapter? How?

5. Read John 15:9–11. What does obedience have to do with joy?

Notes

1. Donald Grey Barnhouse, *Let Me Illustrate* (Grand Rapids: Revell, 1967), 185.
2. Paul Tillich, quoted in Mark Water, comp., *The New Encyclopedia of Christian Quotations* (Grand Rapids: Baker, 2000), 537.
3. Oswald Chambers, *My Utmost for His Highest* (USA: Dodd, Mead & Company, 1935), 244 (August 31).

13

COME TO THE TABLE:
The Solar of Intimacy

We were born with a longing for intimacy of a kind no human relationship will satisfy. The longing is buried deep in every human heart, sometimes overlaid by the fears and traumas that life has taught us. But it burns deep within us still.

JOHN WHITE
Magnificent Obsession

A spiritual kingdom lies all about us, enclosing us, embracing us, altogether within reach of our inner selves, waiting for us to recognize it. God Himself is here waiting our response to His presence.

A. W. TOZER
The Pursuit of God

If anyone loves me, he will obey my teaching. My Father will love him, and we will come to him and make our home with him.

JESUS
John 14:23

When I first met my husband, he was, of course, a stranger to me. Oh, to be sure, I'd been told his name and had seen his blond hair and blue eyes, but what was he like? What interested him? What were his passions? I really knew nothing about him.

After working together for a time (he was a college dorm director while I was a resident assistant), I started discovering things about this man who'd been a mystery to me. He delighted in sunsets but detested summer heat. He enjoyed cooking but not washing the pans. He liked any ice cream but preferred it with pretzels. And though he enjoyed campus ministry, he planned to go to seminary one day. Don intrigued me, and the more I got to know him, the more I found myself doing things I thought would make him smile.

Now, after twenty years of marriage, I just know (well, at least most of the time). I know Don's likes and dislikes. I know his taste in food, clothing, music, authors, and books. More importantly, I know his passions and what brings joy to his heart. Don and I have a relationship marked by intimacy. We share a deep familiarity with each other that is both personal and private, but can be public, too. We *know* each other not just in the physical sense, but in the deepest relational sense humanly possible. As husband and wife, we know and love and are known and loved in return.

Relationship with God can be marked with the same qualities of the best marriage relationships (Ephesians 5), and that includes intimacy. God knows us and wants us to know Him. He loves us and desires our love in return. When we first entered the Fortress, we sought refuge in the things God would provide, but God moved us beyond what He could do for us into the realms of personal knowledge of Him. With each step through the Fortress, we deepened our understanding of who He is and began to see things from His perspective. The result was hope and joy. Now we've come to the innermost room where we draw closest to God.

Drawing close to God isn't anything new. In fact, it seems to be normative for the Christian life. Psalm 73:28 says, "But as for me, it is good to be near God. I have made the Sovereign LORD my refuge." Hebrews 10:22 tells us, "Let us draw near to God with a sincere heart in full assurance of faith." James 4:8 promises, "Come near to God and he will come near to you." Refuge, faith, the promise of reciprocation—these certainly help us draw near, but our best model of intimacy with God is Jesus Himself.

By examining one of Jesus' busiest recorded days (in Mark 6:30–56), we glimpse what it means to walk with God, even on hectic days. Let's look to Jesus, our model.

A MODEL FOR INTIMACY

One of the busiest days recorded in biblical history can be found in Mark 6. Jesus started that day with grief upon hearing that His dear friend and cousin, John the Baptist, had been beheaded (Mark 6:29). Next, He listened to His disciples report on their preaching stints in Galilee (verse 30). All morning long people came and went, so much so, in fact, that Jesus and the disciples had no time to eat (verse 31). Jesus knew they needed rest, so He told the disciples, "Come with me . . . to a quiet place and get some rest" (verse 31). Though they attempted to go to a solitary place, the crowd guessed where they were going and arrived there ahead of them (verse 33). Jesus, in compassion, taught the crowd again. And that was just the morning.

Jesus and the disciples spent the rest of the day teaching and literally hosting a banquet for thousands (verses 34–44). Then, after a long day of ministry, teaching, and performing miracles, though He must have been exhausted, Jesus sent the disciples away, "dismissed the crowd," and withdrew to the mountains to pray (verses 45–46). Even then His middle-of-the-night prayer time was interrupted when had to rescue His seafaring disciples in a storm (verses 47–51).

Lest you think this was an isolated day, the passage tells us that with daybreak, this intense cycle of ministry began all over again (verses 54–56). Jesus essentially pulled an all-nighter (remember those?), and found another needy crowd waiting for Him at dawn. Yet nowhere in this account is Jesus irritable or rushed. (His response is compassion.) Nowhere do we see Him impatient or resentful. Why? Because Jesus didn't rely on His human resources. He relied on His intimacy with God.

Just how intimate was Jesus with the Father? In John 10:30 Jesus declared, "I and the Father are one." On several other occasions, Jesus revealed that He and the Father were one, that apart from the Father He could do nothing, and that He completed only the work that His Father had for Him to do. (See, for example, John 5:19; 10:30; 14:9–11, 31.)

HOW JESUS DEVELOPED INTIMACY WITH THE FATHER

Jesus' relationship with the Father was characterized by oneness and intimacy. What can we learn from Him?

1. *Jesus' intimacy with God was grounded on knowledge.* John 10:15 makes it clear that God knew Jesus and Jesus knew God. They had an intimate knowledge of each other. That was the key to Jesus' understanding of what to do, and not to do, in the course of His busy day. In similar fashion, Jesus knows us, and we are to learn to recognize His voice (John 10:3–5, 14). As He told the Pharisees and others, "I know my sheep and my sheep know me" (John 10:14). The more we know of Him and His ways, the more we will learn to recognize His voice.

2. *Jesus' intimacy with God was marked by dependence.* As He told the religious leaders: "The Son can do nothing by himself; he can do only what he sees his Father doing, because whatever the Father does the Son also does. For the Father loves the Son

and shows him all he does" (John 5:19–20). Jesus was utterly dependent on the Father. He sought God's purposes and pursued God in prayer. When life became particularly intense or demanding, when His ministry was busiest, Jesus retreated for special times of prayer (Mark 1:35; 6:46; 14:32–36). In similar fashion, Jesus tells us that apart from Him we can do nothing (John 15:5). We are every bit as dependent on Him as He was on the Father.

3. *Jesus' time with God took priority over ministry.* Despite the fact that there was still much work to be done, Jesus dismissed the crowd (Mark 6:45). He deliberately and willfully chose to remove Himself from the demands of the day in order to guard His relationship with His Father (Mark 6:46). Despite overwhelming needs, Jesus *stopped* the cycle of busyness and said no to some very important responsibilities in order to say yes to time with God.

4. *Jesus spent private time with God.* In Mark 6:45–46, Jesus separated Himself even from His closest companions. He made the disciples get into the boat, and then He went alone into the mountains to pray. Yes, He did take time away with the disciples on other occasions, but in this case, He went alone. Intimacy with God isn't fostered in a crowd, even in a crowd of friends.

ENTERING THE SOLAR ROOM

I know our journey so far has been primarily about experiencing His refuge in the whirlwind of everyday busyness. But there is a place for withdrawal when we seek refuge. Sometimes, the most effective means of experiencing refuge is undistracted time alone with the Lord of the Fortress. We meet Him most intimately in the Solar.

The solar, by day, was the fortress lord's sitting room; by night, his bedroom. It was a small living room—cozy and warm—a place of quiet far from the noisy crowds below. An open-hearth fireplace heated the room, while tapered candles provided soft, flickering light. To retain heat, tapestries (often displaying historic events or family scenes) lined the solar's walls, and woven rush matting covered the cold stone floors. High-backed chairs, wooden tables, cushions, and a canopied bed completed the solar's furnishings. The solar was designed to foster both conversation and rest.

The solar was also a place of intimacy. Only those closest to the lord could meet with him there. The solar wasn't a place of strategic planning, battle designs, or business meetings; the lord didn't meet with his knights or stewards there. The solar was reserved for loved ones; it was a place of tenderness and vulnerability, a place to know and be known.

The Solar of our Mighty Fortress is much the same. It is reserved for quietness, conversation, tenderness, and vulnerability. Intimacy, both in life and in relationship with God, happens best one-on-one in the most vulnerable places of our souls. God desires that we come to Him in the Solar of Intimacy, even with our hearts' tender places. He invites us to join Him there. Will you come?

COME TO THE TABLE

The Solar table is set for two. The Lord sits waiting for you to meet with Him. No, this isn't a meal-laden table; it is more a table of hushed whispers and inner delight. When you meet with Him here you may find silent awe, a contented soul, a quiet pleasure, or a peace-bathed spirit. Whatever you find, this is a time reserved just for Him and you alone. Here, at this table, in the soft, warm light of the Solar, you are free to enjoy the undistracted company of God.

What is required for this time together? Certainly those things we discovered when we first entered the Fortress: access, trust, and surrender. Like human relationships, it takes love, honesty, and a willingness to be vulnerable (on our part). We also need to know and depend on God, as Jesus did. Perhaps the most difficult requirements to fulfill (in this day and age) are time, privacy, and focus.

MAKING TIME FOR INTIMACY

The first requirement for intimacy, time, is challenging, yet it is more easily found than we realize. When there is an emergency (let's say, for instance, your child breaks his arm, or your mother has a heart attack), everything else falls in line behind that need. The dishes wait. The laundry goes undone. That phone call isn't made, and that women's club meeting has to do without you this time. Emergencies have a way of clarifying our priorities. If we learn to view time with God as necessity (just like a trip to the emergency room for a broken leg or heart attack), we will find the time to be with Him.

Truth be told, we are all enormous time wasters (myself included). TV, magazines, computers (especially addictive computer games), the telephone—how much time do they eat in a day? How much do we feed them? Sometimes we turn to them because we need rest (an important priority), but do they really provide rest?

The more I pursue intimacy with God, the more I'm convinced that lack of time isn't the primary issue. I think the greater issue is that we really don't think relationship with God is a practical priority in our workaday worlds. If we really believed that intimacy with God was as important as eating or breathing or a trip to the emergency room, if we really depended on Him the way Jesus did, I don't think finding time for Him would be that great a problem. If Jesus could do *nothing* on His own, how can we?

FINDING PRIVACY FOR INTIMACY

So much of life is spent around people: people at home; people at work; people at church; people on the bus, on the train, on the plane, or in the store. The same holds true in our Christian lives. We can become involved with Bible study classes, prayer partners, support groups, cell groups, coffee fellowships, Sunday school classes, sewing guilds, and missions boards. Add to these all the committees available, and life can become a crowded place. As we saw in Jesus' life, intimacy doesn't happen in a crowd.

Yes, fellowship is important. Praying together is commanded. But at certain times we need to pray alone. I don't mean emergency prayers or the ongoing abiding prayer we discussed at the Well. I mean, rather, that we must learn to pray "in the closet" where we are face-to-face, alone with God.

The joy about privacy with God is that we don't have to worry about what anyone else thinks! We can be completely honest. We can reveal our deepest, darkest shames. We can admit our fears and confess our sin without self-consciousness. Praying alone is a freeing experience and liberating for the soul.

If praying alone is intimidating, try journaling or praying aloud with your eyes open. I often pray out loud when I'm alone. It keeps me awake (yes, I do occasionally fall asleep when I pray) and it keeps me focused.

The more difficult aspect of praying alone is listening. That part of our private prayer lives becomes easier as we learn to focus.

HAVING FOCUS FOR INTIMACY

Imagine sitting at the Solar's candlelit table gazing into the eyes of the Lover of your soul. Imagine reaching for Him across the table and listening for His tender whispers. Just as He begins to speak . . . the phone rings, the radio blasts, and someone knocks at the door! Not very conducive to intimacy, is it? Yet we often try to meet Him just this way. Classic author Andrew Murray describes our difficulty well:

> Ah! If we would but take time to turn our eyes and hearts away from this world, and from all the loving faces and friends that surround us, and all the joys that attract us, and all the love that greets us, and fix them steadfastly and humbly and trustingly on the face and the love and the joy of Jesus, He is able so to manifest Himself to us that our hearts shall be filled with the consciousness—Jesus is with me. Christ can make His presence as near and as clear and as dear to me as the fellowship of the dearest ones upon earth.[1]

Jesus becomes real to us, and our intimacy grows when we learn to focus on Him. Silence fosters our sense of His presence with us.

Once it's quiet, try meditating on a single attribute of God. Give yourself some part of Him on which to focus. If you have to, write that attribute down and read it again and again. You can do the same with Scripture. Read the Song of Solomon or the Twenty-Third Psalm. If it helps, envision Him sitting with you there.

What do His hands look like? Are they the long-fingered hands of the artist who formed you or the nail-scarred hands of your Savior?

What is the look in His eye? Is it joy, delight, love, and tenderness? Or is it compassion, reproof, sorrow, or pain?

As you meet Him today, is He the Potter, the Shepherd, the Counselor, or King? What does He have to say? Pause for a moment to listen. Don't be afraid of silence.

And don't worry if you get distracted. Silence takes some getting used to (it feels very threatening at first). God will draw you back to Himself. He pursues you even now. Won't you take a moment to sit with Him now in the quiet of the Solar? He's waiting for you there.

⤙ PUTTING IT INTO PRACTICE ⤚

The table to the right summarizes several requirements for and barriers to intimacy with God. (There are others.) It also lists suggestions for fostering intimacy. Look over the chart and reflect on your relationship with God. What is going well? What do you need to change? Then choose one suggestion to foster intimacy and try it this week.

Once you've taken some time to examine your relationship with God, prayerfully ask God to remove any barriers and to increase your oneness with Him.

REQUIREMENTS FOR INTIMACY	BARRIERS TO INTIMACY	SUGGESTIONS FOR FOSTERING INTIMACY
ACCESS TO GOD	SINFUL NATURE	Accept Christ as Savior and confess Him as Lord.
	UNCONFESSED SIN	Confess your sins to God.
FAITHFULNESS	A DIVIDED HEART	Ask God to give you an undivided heart. Repent of those things that have become more important to you than God.
TRUST	NOT KNOWING GOD	Get to know the true God of the Bible.
	BELIEVING THE WRONG THINGS ABOUT GOD	Study God's Word to correct your misconceptions.
	NOT TAKING GOD AT HIS WORD	Choose to believe His Word.
HONESTY	PRETEND PIETY or FALSEHOOD	Remember grace, and be completely truthful with God.
DEPENDENCE	SELF-SUFFICIENCY	Realize your utter dependence on God for *everything* (life, health, breath, finances, etc.); then humble yourself before Him.
TIME	BUSYNESS	Realize that your value, worth, and approval are found in God. View time with God as non-negotiable. Say no to an optional activity, and make time for God.
PRIVACY	CROWDS	Spend time in prayer alone.
FOCUS	NOISE INATTENTION	Turn something off. Find a quiet place to focus on God.

Questions for Reflection

1. Think of someone with whom you are especially close (a best friend or spouse, for example). What is it about your relationship that makes that closeness possible?

2. Now think of your relationship with God. Compare your relationship with Him to the relationship you described in question one. How is it the same? How is it different?

3. Can you identify with the day described in Mark 6 (on page 158)? How?

4. What can you learn from how Jesus handled that day?

5. Of the three barriers to intimacy listed in this chapter—lack of time, privacy, or focus—which is most challenging for you?

Note

1. Andrew Murray, *Absolute Surrender* (Uhrichsville, Ohio: Barbour, 1984), 100.

14

ALL IS WELL:
The Chapel of Peace

*Worship and worry cannot live in the same heart;
they are mutually exclusive.*

RUTH GRAHAM BELL
Prodigals and Those Who Love Them

*Peace I leave with you; my peace I give you. I do not give to you as the
world gives. Do not let your hearts be troubled and do not be afraid.*

JESUS
John 14:27

⊹⊱⊰⊹

You will keep in perfect peace him whose mind is
steadfast, because he trusts in you.

—ISAIAH 26:3

We've come a long way together; our journey is almost done. We've traveled from the castle's outer regions, through inner rooms, and into intimacy with God. Quietly, without notice, while we delighted in God's presence, He has lifted us from the Solar of Intimacy and carried us to the Chapel of Peace.

What is the chapel? Where is it located? A fortress chapel was the highest place in a castle; the masons and builders wanted nothing between their chapel and heaven, nothing between them and their God. It was also situated close to the solar and domestic quarters because the chapel served as the fortress's center of worship. The castle lord and his lady often started the day there in prayer.

The chapel was considered a holy place: a place of reflection and prayer, of song and chant, of ceremony and solitude. It was a place for repentance, forgiveness, confession, and absolution. It was a place of peace and rest for the soul.

It was also a haven for criminals. Medieval cathedrals had the right to give sanctuary; fugitives could flee to the chapel to escape prosecution. Inside each chapel, a heavy iron ring hung on the center of an interior wall. Rebel, felon, murderer, wrongly accused—anyone who made it to the chapel and took hold of the iron ring could claim sanctuary. As long as the fugitive remained in the chapel, he was immune to arrest and prosecution. If he ventured out of the chapel he was subject to accusation, prosecution, and death. Outside, the fugitive lived in fear; inside, he found peace.

As so it is for us. Just as the medieval fugitive found sanctuary and peace in the chapel, we, too, find sanctuary and peace with God.

TEMPORARY SANCTUARY, TEMPORARY PEACE

On a brilliant October day last fall, when autumn leaves peaked with color, we visited Hawk Mountain Sanctuary in Kempton, Pennsylvania. Hawk Mountain is known as the best place on the East Coast (some would say in the world) to watch predatory birds (called raptors) migrate. During the fall's migration season, bird-watchers can see as many as one thousand raptors a day, often at eye level, from any one of several scenic overlooks. Annual migrations bring over a dozen raptor species: everything from sharp-shinned hawks to golden eagles to peregrine falcons. It's an amazing display of God's glory in creation.

Less known is Hawk Mountain Sanctuary's work to protect raptors. Hawk Mountain is a *sanctuary*. It provides protection and refuge for raptors by preserving their habitat, controlling predators, providing nestboxes and nesting platforms, and ensuring proper forestry practices. Hawk Mountain, once known (in the 1920s and early 1930s) as a place of widespread raptor kills, now provides safety and protection for species formerly hunted. On every foot of this twenty-four-hundred-acre preserve, hunting is illegal.

Hawk Mountain, for all its efforts, can only provide temporary sanctuary. It provides safety and peace for the raptors only as long as they stay within the sanctuary's borders. When the birds fly out, they can be hunted and killed.

We are much like the raptors at Hawk Mountain. Though the Chapel is always there, and though its sanctuary is continually available to us, we fly in and out of the Chapel as we follow the course of our lives. Sometimes our hearts are at peace (in the Chapel) and sometimes they are not (outside the Chapel). What's the difference? Fear.

Like the medieval fugitive outside the chapel, we fear many things (though our fears differ from his). We fear crime, inflation, falling stock prices, war, natural disasters, and the unknown. We fear losing a job, losing control, losing others' respect, and losing our health. We fear losing our children, our spouses, our loved ones, and friends. We fear being hurt, abandoned, betrayed, or misunderstood. The things we worry about are the things we fear. Fear is no stranger to us. It robs us of peace.

All too often, we attempt to relieve our fears by looking for peace outside of the Chapel. We may look for peace in people, professionals, and in the latest stress management techniques. We may seek it in drugs, alcohol, shopping, or other addictions that provide momentary escape from our fears. But seeking peace in these avenues is like putting Band-Aids on skin cancer lesions. It may provide a momentary reprieve, but it won't heal. Band-Aids don't treat the root cause.

The root of our inner turmoil isn't really conflict or restlessness. It isn't even fear. We live without peace not because we fear, but because we fear the wrong things.

FEARING THE WRONG THINGS

While we were hiking at Hawk Mountain, I watched a young father and mother trying to reason with their distraught four-year-old daughter.

"I want my baby doll," the preschooler wailed.

"She's back at the car," her mother soothed. "We're going to get her."

"We have to walk this way," her father gently explained, pointing down the tree-lined trail.

"But . . . I waa-nnt my baby," the little girl sniffled.

"Sweetie, to get your baby doll, we have to walk down this path just a little ways. Mommy and Daddy will help you. And then we'll find your baby back at the car."

"But I can't go that way; it's too faaa-aarrrr." The child continued to cry. "And I'm thirsty and I wanna drink."

"The water is back at the car, too. You need to come this way to get your baby and to get a drink. You can do it; we'll help you. Now, let's go."

"But I caa-aaaan't. I don't like this path. I can't go without my baaa-by." With her silky blond hair hanging over her tear-streaked face, she folded her arms, sat down, and cried harder. She wouldn't budge.

This little girl was completely without peace. Why? Because she feared the wrong things. She feared not having her baby doll. She feared the path ahead. She feared that the car was too far away and that she just couldn't make it. She didn't focus on the one thing that could've provided her peace: her parents. She didn't believe what they told her; she didn't trust that their plan was good, and she didn't obey when they told her to come.

I had to chuckle as I watched this pint-sized illustration of a life without peace. She was so much like me. How often am I "peaceless" because I fear the path my Father has chosen? How often do I rob myself of peace because I fear what I don't have? How often do I fear what will be required of me or what lies ahead? I deny myself the opportunity to experience God's peace because I fear my circumstances instead of fearing the God who rules my circumstances.

FEARING GOD

The Bible actually tells us to fear God. Deuteronomy 10:12 says, "And now, O Israel, what does the LORD your God ask of you but to fear the LORD your God, to walk in all his ways, to love him, to serve the LORD your God with all your heart and with all your soul." A few verses later, the passage adds, "Fear the LORD your God and serve him. Hold fast to him and take your oaths in his name" (verse 20). The writer of Ecclesiastes affirms this idea: "Fear God and keep his commandments, for this is the whole duty of man" (Ecclesiastes 12:13).

Fearing God for the Christian is not a feeling of dread or terror; it isn't cowering before Him or being afraid of His wrath. It's more a matter of recognizing God as God and responding with worship, trust, and obedience. To fear God means that we respond to His character with reverence. It means that we believe that God is worthy of our worship and loyalty. If we fear God (revere His name), we will trust Him and obey His Word. Fearing God, as it's described in the Bible, results in peace.

FINDING BIBLICAL PEACE

The Bible has a lot to say about peace:

- God is the source of our peace (Psalm 29:11).
- Peace results from loving God's Law (Psalm 119:165).
- Peace is a byproduct of trust (Isaiah 26:3; Romans 8:6; 15:13).
- Peace is a fruit of righteousness (Isaiah 32:17).
- Peace is related to obedience (Isaiah 48:18).
- Peace is a fruit of the Holy Spirit (Galatians 5:22).
- Jesus Himself is our peace and provides peace (Ephesians 2:14; 2 Thessalonians 3:16).

Several of these passages summarize what it means to fear God. We fear God by loving His Law and obeying His commands. We fear God by trusting Him. We fear God by walking in righteousness. We fear God by looking to Jesus as our source of peace and finding peace in Him. When we fear God, we experience peace.

BEING ROBBED OF PEACE

If we considered *all* the dynamics of fearing God, all the facets of our relationships with Him, *and all* the potential sources of other fears, we could write an entire book on how to experience peace. But this book is about finding refuge. The ways to experience peace that we will examine here will focus on circumstances in which we are most likely to seek refuge (there are many more). In my work in women's ministry and in my own life, I've noticed three chronic challenges that can rob us of peace: self-accusation, overwhelming circumstances, and disobedience.

First, we accuse ourselves. We accuse ourselves because we fear God's punishment, fear failure, or fear what others think.

How can we experience peace when our thoughts accuse us?

Remember what Christ has done for us. First John 5:11 assures us that "God has given us eternal life, and this life is in his Son." That life can never be taken away (John 10:28). In this sense, we find permanent sanctuary in the Mighty Fortress of God.

Unlike the temporary sanctuary of the Chapel, God gave us permanent sanctuary when we crossed the Drawbridge of Faith. We, in effect, took hold of the iron ring of Christ's righteousness. We laid claim to His sanctuary and became forever immune to punishment. Jesus, remember, took the punishment we deserved and gave us His righteousness (see chapter 1). God provides permanent sanctuary in Jesus, and when we enter that sanctuary, we never leave.

If Jesus is our permanent sanctuary, we, like the medieval fugitive, need not fear.

"There is no fear in love. But perfect love drives out fear, because fear has to do with punishment" (1 John 4:18). We can now live at peace, forever, with God (Romans 5:1). In other words, once we've been given sanctuary in Jesus Christ, it is ours for eternity. Don't be confused here; Jesus *never* lets go.

Our problem is that we forget. We let go of the ring. We lose our peace in the wake of self-accusation and self-condemning thoughts. The camcorders of our minds play and replay every mistake, failure, sin, or guilt-inducing regret. We forget Christ's righteousness (though it is still ours) and expect to be condemned. We live in fear.

While true guilt over sin (the conviction God's Holy Spirit brings) drives us back to God (we discovered this on the Staircase in chapter 8), many of us live with chronic, condemning, false guilt that robs us of peace and drives us away from Him. This kind of guilt comes from our adversary, Satan, the Accuser, and has no place in the believer's life. When facing this kind of guilt, take hold once again of the iron ring in the Chapel. Remember your permanent sanctuary there, and recall that Jesus never lets go.

Second, we let circumstances overwhelm us. The reason? We fear that life is out of control. We often seek refuge in God when events push us beyond our ability to control or make sense of them. Life *feels* overwhelming and we lose our peace.

The antidote for this kind of fear is worship.

One March morning, while lingering in that semiconscious state between wakefulness and sleep, I kept hearing the same word: "awesome . . . awesome . . . awesome." Thinking that maybe I'd spent too much time preparing for this chapter, I didn't pay much attention until I realized that I wasn't dreaming. I really did hear voices! My radio alarm woke me to coverage of local response to a professional basketball game played the night before.

The interviewees were responding to the first game of the 2001 NBA Championship finals. The Los Angeles Lakers, having won an unprecedented nineteen games straight, including eleven playoff games, were expected to sweep the series and take the national title. It didn't happen. In the previous night's game the underdog Philadelphia 76ers defeated the Lakers 107 to 101 in overtime.

In interviews around Philadelphia the next morning, people used one word to describe 76er's Alan Iverson's performance. "Awesome," said one woman in the interview. "He was just awesome," enthused another. "Scoring 48 points . . . wow! Alan was awesome," gushed a third. I wasn't hallucinating. I really did hear the word "awesome" repeated during the interviews!

As I woke up listening to person after person praise the performance of a basketball player, I couldn't help but wonder why we so readily revere athletic performance, but find it difficult to worship God.

It may be that we no longer fear Him. In our quest to know God as loving Father, merciful Savior, and "friend," we sometimes miss the reverence due His name. For us to experience the peace that comes from refuge in God, we must believe that God is bigger than we are and worthy of our praise. When was the last time we bowed to God's holiness? Have we been speechless over His majesty? How long since we stood in awe before His greatness? How big is our God, really?

Nineteenth century Quaker preacher and Harvard-trained scholar Thomas Kelly wrote, "The basic response of the soul to [God] is internal adoration and joy, thanksgiving and worship, self-surrender and listening. The secret places of the heart . . . become a holy sanctuary of adoration and self-oblation, where we are kept in perfect peace if our minds be stayed on Him."[1]

Do you see the connection among the bigness of God, worship, and peace? Worship is simply our heart's response to the almighty God of our refuge; it is an attitude of devotion that sings of His majesty and glory and stands in awe before His greatness.

To remain in the chapel, to continually experience the peace of its sanctuary, we must keep our hearts and minds focused on who God is and worship Him accordingly. Then we can say with the psalmist, "I will lie down and sleep in peace, for you alone, O LORD, make me dwell in safety" (Psalm 4:8). When we worship God, our hearts can be at peace.

Third, we are robbed of peace when we disobey God. We disobey when we fear that God's way may not be the best way.

When I think of the little girl on the trail at Hawk Mountain, I wonder how different her experience might have been had she "feared" her parents— meaning she had recognized who her parents were, trusted them, and obeyed their direction. The family car was an easy five-minute walk down the wooded, cedar-chipped path. If she'd trusted her parents, she could've had a peaceful heart, and, for the time it took her to protest, she could've been at the car holding her baby and drinking her water. Instead, she remained upset and miserable on the trail.

Part of fearing God means that we will worship and trust Him. But it also means we will obey Him. The Bible tells us that God's ways (the ways of wisdom) "are pleasant ways, and all [His] paths are peace" (Proverbs 3:17). When we follow God's ways, we will experience peace.

The prophet Isaiah, as the voice of God to Israel, cried out to Israel, "If only you had paid attention to [God's] commands, your peace would have been like a river" (Isaiah 48:18). The Psalms tell us that those who love (and obey) God's law have great peace (Psalm 119:165). Even the apostle Paul links obedience with peace: "Whatever you have learned or received or heard from me, or seen in me—put it into practice. And the God of peace will be with you" (Philippians 4:9).

The more we know of who God is and what He desires of us, and the more we follow His paths, the greater our peace will be.

Fellow traveler, what do you fear? What robs you of peace? Won't you return to the Chapel and find freedom from fear in the God of all peace? His Chapel is always open. He welcomes you now.

-⊰ PUTTING IT INTO PRACTICE ⊱-

Twentieth-century writer Thomas Merton said, "We are not at peace with others because we are not at peace with ourselves, and we are not at peace with ourselves because we are not at peace with God."[2]

Take time now to reflect on the condition of your soul. Are you at peace? Why or why not? If not, visualize yourself entering the Chapel and grasping the iron ring of Christ's righteousness in your hand. Know that the sanctuary you have in Christ's righteousness covers you for eternity.

Now think about the greatness of God. Consider what you've learned about God in your refuge journey. How does knowing the God of this Fortress give you peace?

Questions for Reflection

1. From what do you need sanctuary?

2. What kind of self-accusations do you most often face?

3. How does Jesus give us peace in the midst of those accusations?

4. What are you tempted to fear more than God?

5. What is your response to Isaiah 26:3?

Notes

1. Thomas Kelly, *Devotional Classics: Selected Readings for Individuals and Groups,* eds. Richard J. Foster and James Bryan Smith (San Francisco: Harper, 1993), 206.
2. Thomas Merton, quoted in Mark Water, comp., *The New Encyclopedia of Christian Quotations* (Grand Rapids: Baker, 2000), 719.

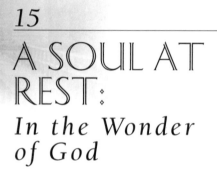

15

A SOUL AT REST:
In the Wonder of God

True religion is a union of the soul with God.

HENRY SCOUGAL
The Life of God in the Soul of Man

⇥✦⇤

My soul finds rest in God alone; my salvation comes from him.
He alone is my rock and my salvation; he is my fortress, I will
never be shaken. Trust in him at all times, O people; pour out
your hearts to him, for God is our refuge.

—PSALM 62:1–2, 8

Such knowledge is too wonderful for me.

—PSALM 139:6

When I started this chapter, life had come to a standstill. The United States was under attack by a faceless enemy with unknown support and an unknown agenda. The Pentagon was burning in Washington. Over five thousand people were feared trapped beneath what remained of New York City's Twin Towers. Two hundred sixty-six passengers and crew from four hijacked planes were dead. Citizens feared more attacks might be coming.

Our government reacted swiftly, closing the nation's airports and public monuments. The nation went to the highest level of security alert since World War II. The Federal Aviation Administration grounded every aircraft; not a single commercial or private plane crossed American skies. All these measures, however, did little to ease our misgivings. We still wondered, *Will they strike again? Where? How many more will die?*

In a single morning our sense of security went from confidence to uncertainty, and life as we knew it changed before our eyes.

I began this chapter only two days after the September 11, 2001, terrorist attacks on the United States of America. Our nation reeled in disbelief, grief, and outrage. Many were numb. Those directly affected were frantic over missing loved ones or deeply grieving those confirmed dead. The rest of us grieved with them, even as we grieved the loss of our sense of security in a more uncertain world. Oh, how we needed refuge.

Refuge. What does it really mean? This book has looked at finding refuge in the Mighty Fortress of God. We have discussed the requirements and results of refuge—faith, trust, surrender, relief, comfort, renewal, and provision. We saw the impact refuge had on us—growth, strength, eternal perspective, and hope. We also have explored the benefits refuge has on our relationships with God— joy, intimacy, and peace. But when it really counts, when life becomes threatening and uncertain or when our worlds crumble, does refuge in God really make any difference at all?

You bet it does. Listen to Psalm 62:1–8:

My soul finds rest in God alone; my salvation comes from him. He alone is my rock and my salvation; he is my fortress, I will never be shaken. . . . Find rest, O my soul, in God alone; my hope comes from him. He alone is my rock and my salvation; he is my fortress, I will not be shaken. My salvation and my honor depend on God; he is my mighty rock, my refuge. Trust in him at all times, O people; pour out your hearts to him, for God is our refuge.

FINDING REST IN GOD ALONE

Do you hear it? "My soul finds rest in God alone. . . . He alone is my rock. . . . I will never be shaken." God *alone* is our rock. God *alone* is our rest. God *alone* keeps us from shaking. Refuge in God makes a difference because it is the only place in this world where our souls can rest. His refuge stills our hearts and calms our fears, even when the world crashes around us.

When Pharaoh's army trapped God's people at the banks of the Red Sea, Moses exhorted his people to stand firm and to watch for God's deliverance. He told them, "The Lord will fight for you; you need only to be still" (Exodus 14:14). The Israelites must have thought, *Are you crazy? Be still in the face of an advancing army bent on annihilation? Be still when there is no way out?* Yet, God answers, "Be still."

David, when contrasting the wicked and the righteous, exhorts us in Psalm 37:7, "Be still before the LORD and wait patiently for him; do not fret when men succeed in their ways, when they carry out their wicked schemes."

We're tempted to think, *Are you nuts? Be still when evil prospers?*

Be still when our enemies appear to succeed? "Yes," God says, "Be still."
Be still when a loved one has a stroke and is never the same? "Be still."
Be still when a spouse dies and we're fractured with grief? "Be still."
Be still when we can't make the deadline and might lose our job? "Be still."
Be still when a child rejects us or turns from our faith? "Be still."
Be still when we're weary from busyness and see no way out? "Be still."
Be still when we're confused and broken and don't understand? "Yes, even then, be still."

"Be still, and know that I am God," says the Lord of the Fortress. "I will be exalted among the nations, I will be exalted in the earth" (Psalm 46:10).

Stillness comes when we understand that God is God and there is no other (Deuteronomy 4:35). Stillness comes when we realize no plan of His can be thwarted (Job 42:2). Stillness comes when we run to God's waiting arms and cast ourselves on His mercy. It comes when we're sure of God's sovereignty and certain of His goodness. It comes when we realize there is nowhere else to turn, and hide beneath His wings. Stillness comes when we entrust ourselves to the God of this Fortress.

"Be still," He whispers. "I am your refuge."

REFUGE IN HIS SHADOW

I have to admit that I struggled while writing this book. When I started the manuscript, I thought I had some idea of what biblical refuge really was. The process of writing, however, produced far more questions for me than answers. It seemed like the more I studied, the less I understood. The more I researched, the more incomprehensible God became. This was especially true after our teaching trip to Africa and in the aftermath of the terrorists' attacks. Too many things made no sense to me.

It wasn't that my trust in God was shattered; I held firm to the belief that God still ruled from His throne. And it wasn't even that I doubted who God was; He was still good and righteous in all His ways. It was more that I couldn't reconcile the idea of refuge in Him with the world I saw around me.

The ambiguity was awful. God became more of a mystery to me. He didn't fit in my tidy theological boxes anymore. The idea of refuge wasn't as clear as it used to be, and I began to wonder if I really knew God at all.

This was a good thing. You see, God was driving me to a deeper refuge than I'd ever experienced. He was teaching me to find refuge in Him, even when it was God Himself—His bigness and the complete incomprehensibility of His ways—that drove me to seek refuge.

God became my refuge in the face of countless unanswered questions. I found myself on my knees before a God I knew far less than I'd imagined, but who drew me to Himself nonetheless. Like Job, I felt like I'd heard of God, but now I'd seen Him (Job 42:5), and there was no alternative but to repent and be still.

Psalm 91:1–2 says, "He who dwells in the shelter of the Most High will rest in the shadow of the Almighty. I will say of the LORD, 'He is my refuge and my fortress, my God, in whom I trust.'" Like the psalmist, I found rest in the shadow of the Almighty, even when His shadow hid things about Him and I didn't understand.

My story, however, doesn't end there. In repentance and stillness I discovered one final result of refuge, and it took me completely by surprise. What was it? Wonder.

THE WONDER OF OUR REFUGE

"How great is God—beyond our understanding!" (Job 36:26). Our God is a wonder-full God. In the face of His wonder, "the wisdom of the wise will perish, the intelligence of the intelligent will vanish" (Isaiah 29:14). As I rested beneath this God I couldn't grasp, my wisdom turned out to be not very wise, and what intelligence I thought I had seemed to vanish. Humbled before Him, and with my heart finally still, I caught a glimpse of His wonder. I began to see Him with the wide, round eyes of a child. I no longer had to figure it all out. I no longer needed the answers. I no longer came as an author, teacher, student, or skeptic. I was simply His little girl who looked to Him with childlike trust and amazement.

God's ways astounded and confounded me, but they became a delight to my soul. Oh, the wonder of it all.

There, in the shadow of the Almighty, my confusion turned to wonder, which then turned to praise. My heart cried out with the psalmist:

> I will sing of your strength, in the morning I will sing of your love; for you are my fortress, my refuge in times of trouble. O my Strength, I sing praise to you; you, O God, are my fortress, my loving God. (Psalm 59:16–17)

Where are you on your refuge journey? Do you feel like you've only begun? Don't be discouraged; that's the way of it on this path through the Mighty Fortress of God. The God in whom we take refuge is the great "I AM," who was, and is, and always will be. He is unsearchable (Romans 11:33). "His ways are eternal" (Habakkuk 3:6). What we learn of His refuge in this life is but a poor reflection of the eternal refuge we'll discover when we meet Him face-to-face. We can say with Paul, "Now [we] know in part; then [we] shall know fully, even as [we are] fully known" (1 Corinthians 13:12).

In the meantime, press on. See this journey through to its life-long end. My prayer is that the Lord of this Fortress will make Himself known to you, that He will fill you with wonder, and that He might satisfy your soul like never before.

May God make you faithful to pursue Him, and may you find refuge in Him all the days of your life. Though the journey continues, life goes on, but because of His refuge, we can rest.

-≺- PUTTING IT INTO PRACTICE -≻-

*Read the following psalm, not for information, but with
the wonder-filled eyes of a child. As often as you need to in
the months and years to come, come back to this psalm. You'll
find a renewed sense of refuge in the Mighty Fortress of God
each time you return.*

Psalm 46

*God is our refuge and strength, an ever-present help in trouble.
Therefore we will not fear, though the earth give way and the
mountains fall into the heart of the sea,
though its waters roar and foam
and the mountains quake with their surging.
There is a river whose streams make glad the city of God,
the holy place where the Most High dwells.
God is within her, she will not fall; God will help her at break of day.
Nations are in uproar, kingdoms fall;
he lifts his voice, the earth melts.
The LORD Almighty is with us;
the God of Jacob is our fortress.
Come and see the works of the LORD,
the desolations he has brought on the earth.
He makes wars cease to the ends of the earth;
he breaks the bow and shatters the spear,
he burns the shields with fire.
"Be still, and know that I am God;
I will be exalted among the nations,
I will be exalted in the earth."
The LORD Almighty is with us;
the God of Jacob is our fortress.*

GLOSSARY

bailey. An open, grassy expanse found behind the castle walls; a courtyard.

banner. The flag flown above a fortress depicting the lord's family crest, coat of arms, or other symbols representing the character or reign of the fortress lord.

barbican. A narrow, walled passage making up part of the gatehouse defense.

chapel. That part of the castle that served as its center of worship.

curtain wall. Large, permanent walls surrounding the fortress that spanned the gap between its towers.

drawbridge. A moveable bridge spanning the moat that could be raised or lowered to prevent or provide access to the fortress.

gatehouse. The main entrance to a castle, usually made up of both a barbican and a portcullis.

great hall. Large banquet room used for celebrations and entertainment.

joust. A contest between two knights in which each, while riding at a full gallop and using a variety of weapons, attempted to knock the other off his horse.

keep. A large defensive tower, usually rectangular or square, found in the center or rear of the fortress.

lord. The owner or ruler of the castle.

moat. A defensive ditch surrounding the fortress, usually filled with water.

parapet. A walkway along the top of the curtain walls and towers that sentries used to keep watch of surrounding terrain.

portcullis. A heavy, vertical iron grill that could be lowered to seal off a castle entrance.

sanctuary. A protection afforded in medieval chapels by which an accused criminal could enter the chapel, take hold of an iron ring on the chapel wall, and claim immunity from prosecution.

siege. An enemy's blockade of a fortress designed to force occupants of the fortress to surrender.

solar. The lord's private chambers, usually a large living room in a tower.

storehouse. A cool, dry room used for storing food and supplies.

tapestry. A woven wall-hanging depicting historic scenes or events, often hung to retain heat in the castle.

tower. A castle structure, usually circular or square, which contained a stairwell and connected the fortress's curtain walls, strategically placed at a corner or along the curtain wall of the fortress to offer a commanding view of surroundings and aid in protection against attacks.

well. Essential and primary source of water for the fortress.